100

THINGS TO DO IN
LOS ANGELES
BEFORE YOU
DIE

...dition

D1089682

100

THINGS TO DO IN
LOS ANGELES
BEFORE YOU
DIE

· ·

DANNY JENSEN AND CARRIE KIM

Library of Congress Control Number: 2017958796

ISBN: 9781681061337

Design by Jill Halpin

Printed in the United States of America
18 19 20 21 22   5 4 3 2 1

Please note that websites, phone numbers, addresses, and company names are subject to
change or cancellation. We did our best to relay the most accurate information available, but
due to circumstances beyond our control, please do not hold us liable for misinformation.
When exploring new destinations, please do your homework before you go.

DEDICATION

Danny:

To Adrienne, my love and fellow adventurer.

Carrie:

To my parents, Larry & Mary Anne Facey,
who've fostered my sense of adventure and have
shown me there's always something new to do.

CONTENTS

• •

• •

Art and Entertainment

• •

• •

Culture and History

• •

PREFACE

Los Angeles has it all. Seriously. We have beaches and mountains. We make movies and television. We have history, diversity, art, music, and a food scene that spans five-star restaurants and food trucks. Yeah, we've got some traffic and the seasons hardly change, but no one here seems to mind year-round sunshine.

Los Angeles's sprawling city limits are exciting, but can be intimidating as well. It's easy to get overwhelmed by the possibilities or get stuck in a rut and forget about all the cool things there are to do. But we can't have you lying on your deathbed wishing you'd visited the Magic Castle or seen just one movie inside the Cinerama Dome, now can we?

Three things to keep in mind:

1. Things are always changing in L.A. Sometimes our favorite places can disappear overnight. We've tried to stick with quintessential Los Angeles spots that have stood the test of time, but we've also chosen destinations that demonstrate just how diverse the city is, both culturally and culinarily. So do a bit of research in advance before you check them out in person.

2. We're not neighborhood snobs. Pasadena counts as L.A. in this book, as does the South Bay. Basically, if it's in Los Angeles County, it's fair game. Although our take on Los Angeles may span farther than some L.A. purists' views (oh yes, L.A. purists exist—and they're hardcore), we didn't get crazy

• •

and mention Disneyland or anything. Because come on, Orange County is NOT Los Angeles.

3. While you may find places and activities in this book that are popular with both locals and tourists, we tried to steer clear of anything that's covered extensively by other L.A. guides. We want to push you a little farther toward those out-of-the-way gems that you've maybe heard about but never had a chance to try and also to discover places you never knew existed. We love nothing better than to hear a long-time Angeleno say, "How did I not know about this amazing place?"

Though we've both lived here for many years, we fell a little deeper in love with L.A. while writing this book, and we didn't think that was possible. We hope you'll do the same. Enjoy it and keep in touch, will you? We love talking about Los Angeles so much we have a Facebook page where we can share even more wonderful discoveries (100ThingsLA). Stop by and share your experiences. See you on the 405, friends.

• •

ACKNOWLEDGMENTS

Danny:

Special thanks to the members of my tremendously supportive family who have always encouraged me to follow my dreams and taught me to love the lifelong adventure of learning. Thanks to my wonderful friends for joining me to explore far-flung corners of L.A. Special gratitude goes to the Nine Hundy family of friends for making Los Angeles a home for me. Thanks to Carrie Kim for inviting me along for the 2nd edition, and thanks to Jeff Miller for encouraging me to dig deeper into the stories of the city that he so loves.

Carrie:

Writing a book about a city as big as Los Angeles is no easy task! Thanks to all the readers, both locals and those who were just visiting, who helped make the 1st edition of this book so successful that it warranted an update. A sincere and special thanks also goes out to Danny Jensen for coming onboard to create this 2nd edition and giving me almost a whole new list to conquer!

• •

FOOD AND DRINK

GRAB A BURGER AND PIE
AT THE APPLE PAN

Get into a debate about L.A.'s best burger, and The Apple Pan will make it to the final round every time. The cozy diner is old-fashioned in the most authentic way, and there are absolutely no retro gimmicks (like at Johnny Rocket's, the 1940s-style chain, which took its inspiration from here).

Keeping things simple, there are just two kinds of burgers, five sandwiches, and three different pies. French fries, coffee, and soda are the obvious supporting roles on the menu. For extra cool points, you can also order a few special off-the-menu items, including a tuna melt, cheese fries, a lettuce-wrapped burger (for the gluten-averse), and a root beer float. Heads up: Be prepared to wait; the U-shaped counter surrounding the kitchen only has 26 stools. This also means that you shouldn't attempt rolling in with a huge crew. Last but not least—sweet tooth or not—don't you dare leave there without a taste of that apple pie.

10801 W Pico Blvd., Los Angeles 90064

Neighborhood: West L.A.
Kid friendly

SIP A PERFECT MARTINI
AT MUSSO & FRANK

The oldest restaurant in Hollywood, The Musso & Frank Grill has been an essential L.A. destination since 1919. And the perfectly poured martini is just one of the reasons people keep coming back. Step into this wonderfully charming time warp of a restaurant and make your way to the bar where you'll find a distinguished barman in a red jacket and bowtie who has been pouring for decades. Order up a signature martini, made with gin or vodka and a splash of vermouth, stirred (of course), and served with an adorable little decanter on ice for when you need a refresher. Take a sip and you'll soon understand why everyone from Charlie Chaplin and Marilyn Monroe to Keith Richards and Harrison Ford—not to mention literary giants like Faulkner and Steinbeck—have passed more than a few hours here.

6667 Hollywood Blvd., Los Angeles 90028
mussoandfrank.com

Neighborhood: Hollywood
Adults only (unless you're eating in the restaurant section)

TIP
If you're in need of a bite, consider grabbing a seat in one of the red leather booths and ordering up some hearty, classic fare like steak and chops from the grill, chicken pot pie, or the Welsh rarebit.

TEST YOUR SPICE TOLERANCE
IN THAI TOWN

L.A. is home to the only officially designated Thai Town in the country, and the six-block stretch in East Hollywood is a great place to test your tolerance for spicy chilies and discover excellent eats beyond just Pad Thai. Most of the restaurants can be found along Hollywood and Sunset boulevards from Western to Normandie Avenues, demarcated by two statues of apsonsi, a mythical angel of Thai folklore that's half-human, half-lion. Jitlada is great place to start, known for its fiery Southern Thai curries and off-menu "Jazz" burger named for the co-owner. Ruen Pair is another of our favorites, and for pungent noodle soups like Boat Noodles, try Sapp Coffee Shop. For breakfast, try the Chinese donuts and savory porridge at Siam Sunset, and for sweets, check out Bhan Kanom Thai.

Jitlada
5233 Sunset Blvd., Los Angeles 90027
jitladala.wordpress.com

Neighborhood: East Hollywood
Kid friendly status is all up to you, parents.

POP TOPS
AT A ONE-OF-A-KIND SODA SHOP

Forget the debate between Coke and Pepsi—there's a small grocery store in the neighborhood of Highland Park where you can find more than 750 varieties of independently produced sodas, many of which you won't find anywhere else. Once a neighborhood Italian grocery store that opened in 1897, Galco's Soda Pop Stop features rows of shelves stocked primarily with unique sodas, plus craft beers and old-fashioned candies.

The store features cult classic sodas like Faygo from Detroit and deli favorite Dr. Brown's, plus fun and eclectic flavors like peach, cucumber, lavender, blueberry, butterscotch, and more. Some brands date back to the 19th century while others are from new artisanal producers. The shop's cheerful owner, John Nese, is always on hand to make recommendations. There's also a station in the back where you can create and bottle your own sodas and a deli with massive "Blockbuster" sandwiches, perfect for pairing with your new favorite soda selections.

Galco's Soda Pop Shop
5702 York Blvd., Los Angeles 90042
galcos.com

Neighborhood: Highland Park
Kid friendly

CROWN THE KING
OF THE FRENCH DIP SANDWICH

Los Angeles is home to two legendary old-school eateries that both claim to have invented the French Dip. Both established in 1908, Philippe the Original and Cole's exist approximately 1.5 miles from each other, and although they offer similar menus, they couldn't be more different. Philippe's is a walk-up-to-the-counter-and-order kind of joint that is bright, bustling, and always busy. Cole's is located on the ground floor of the historic Pacific Electric Building and is dark, old-timey, and has a full bar. Both have droves of loyal fans, so to orchestrate your own face-off be sure to order the same type of sandwich at each place (Beef, Lamb, Pork, or Turkey) to declare your own winner.

Cole's
118 E 6th St.
Los Angeles 90014
colesfrenchdip.com

Philippe the Original
1001 N Alameda St.
Los Angeles 90012
philippes.com

Neighborhood: Downtown
Kid friendly

TIP
Bring your camera with you to the men's restroom at Cole's—there's an elegant plaque declaring which urinal legendary poet Charles Bukowski used! (Ladies, you'll need a camera and a male friend to take the photo for you.)

GET KITSCHY
IN THE BIRTHPLACE OF TIKI CULTURE

Los Angeles is credited as the place where America's Tiki craze began, starting in 1934 with Don the Beachcomber in Hollywood. And while many of the legendary bars and restaurants have long since disappeared, there are still a few classic spots (and some new ones) in L.A. still serving up sweetly potent, typically rum-fueled Tiki drinks and Polynesian-inspired kitsch. Opened in 1958, the laid-back Tonga Hut is the oldest one operating and a great place to grab a stupefying Zombie or share a massive Scorpion Bowl in one of its cozy booths. The small and family-owned Tiki-Ti, which opened in 1961, is another excellent option where you'll find a lengthy menu of boozy drinks and funky tchotchkes everywhere you look. Just try to get there early for a seat.

Tonga Hut
12808 Victory Blvd., North Hollywood 91606
tongahut.com

Tiki-Ti
4427 Sunset Blvd., Los Angeles 90027
tiki-ti.compages/home.html

Neighborhood: North Hollywood and Silver Lake
Adults only

DIVE INTO
THE DELICIOUS REVIVAL OF CHINATOWN

Chinatown is once again an exciting dining destination after years of being taken for granted, thanks to a new wave of creative young chefs. Stroll through iconic courtyards adorned by strings of red lanterns and work up an appetite exploring new art galleries.

Far East Plaza is home to many of the eclectic newcomers and classic standbys. Celebrity chef Roy Choi's Chego serves hearty rice bowls, Howlin' Ray's fires up Nashville hot chicken, LASA offers innovative Filipino cuisine, and Lao Tao serves Taiwanese street food. Kim Chuy has been popular for Teochew-style noodles and leek cakes since 1982.

Other great Chinatown eats include NYC chef David Chang's Majordomo for upscale Korean-inspired fare, Blossom and Pho 87 for Vietnamese food, Yang Chow for classic Chinatown eats, and The Little Jewel of New Orleans for po' boys. General Lee's serves creative cocktails and Melody Lounge pours craft beers.

Far East Plaza
727 N Broadway
Los Angeles 90012

Neighborhood: Chinatown
Kid friendly
(except for the bars)

TIP
Explore Far East Plaza during Chinatown After Dark—which features food from chefs in the plaza, culinary collaborations, and live music—on the first Thursday of every month from 6 pm to 10 pm.

EAT INSECTS AND MOLE
AT GUELAGUETZA

No bucket list would be complete without an adventurous meal of insects, and this beloved, James Beard Award–winning Oaxacan restaurant in Koreatown is the place to take the dare. Guelaguetza is well-known for its excellent moles, traditional Oaxacan sauces made with a myriad of ground chilies and spices, and other specialties like chiles rellenos, platters of tasajo beef, and tlayudas (essentially Oaxacan pizzas). But don't leave without trying the Chapulines a la Mexicana, a stew of sautéed grasshoppers with jalapeños, tomatoes, onions, served with avocado, Oaxacan string cheese, and fresh corn tortillas. Don't be squeamish: the grasshoppers offer a bold, briny, and earthy flavor, plus they come with bragging rights. You can also order sun-dried chapulines seasoned with lime and garlic that have a satisfying crunch.

Guelaguetza
3014 W Olympic Blvd., Los Angeles 90006
ilovemole.com

Neighborhood: Koreatown
Kid friendly

MEET
AT THIRD & FAIRFAX
FOR THE ORIGINAL FARMERS MARKET

People have been saying "Meet me at Third & Fairfax" since 1934, so its billing as "The Original" Farmers Market isn't just a marketing ploy. Yeah, it's a little touristy in parts, but pretend like you didn't see all the cheesy gift shops in the center and keep your focus on the food. There are family-run stands with produce available seven days a week, several gourmet grocers, and a labyrinth of food vendor stalls that represent a genuine microcosm of L.A. diversity.

Don't leave until you've tried the Mee Goreng, a savory pan-fried noodle dish from Singapore's Banana Leaf, and send a friend to grab the Chicken Shawerma Sandwich (don't forget a side of Hamous!) from Moishe's. No time for lunch? Make the obligatory stop at Bob's Coffee and Doughnuts. Just get there. Until you've gone to the Original Farmers Market on Third & Fairfax, you can't really say you've been in L.A.

6333 W 3rd St., Los Angeles 90036
farmersmarketla.com

Neighborhood: Fairfax
Kid friendly

TIP

The Grove, a super trendy and upscale outdoor mall, is also located adjacent to the Farmers Market. It's pretty polarizing: you either love its presence or hate it. It's too major to go unmentioned, and at the very least, it's a great place to stroll through and work off a little of that food you just feasted on at the Farmers Market.

JIGGLE JELL-O AND SIP COCKTAILS
AT CLIFTON'S

Towering redwood trees, wildlife taxidermy, hidden bars, and lots of colorful Jell-O: just some of what's in store at the iconic Clifton's, a decades-old L.A. institution that recently received a spectacular facelift. Originally opened in 1931, Clifton's cafeteria has fed Angelenos for generations (famously feeding those who couldn't pay during the Depression) and its elaborate California-themed décor is said to have even inspired Walt Disney to open a certain theme park. Once there were several Clifton's, each with a different theme, but now only the Downtown location remains, and it's an essential L.A. destination. Start by dropping a coin in the wishing well, then grab a bite at the cafeteria for improved renditions of comfort classics (think prime rib, mac and cheese, and, yes, Jell-O). From there, make your way to one of numerous stylish bars, including the Gothic Bar, The Monarch, and the hidden, Tiki-themed Pacific Seas.

Clifton's Republic
648 S Broadway, Los Angeles 90014
cliftonsla.com

Neighborhood: Downtown
Kid friendly (except for the bars)

EAT SUSHI
ATOP A MOUNTAIN PALACE

There are plenty of incredible sushi destinations in L.A., but none can rival the views from Yamashiro in Hollywood. The iconic hilltop restaurant, built in 1914, was inspired by a mountain palace near Kyoto, Japan. While the courtyard inside the ornately designed wood building is impressive, it's really the sweeping views of the city from the terraced Japanese gardens outside that are a must-see. There you'll also find a 600-year-old pagoda from Japan and a shimmering pool (sorry, no late-night swims). While the sushi and Asian fusion fare won't impress any purists (there are a lot of flashy rolls), and it can get a bit pricy, it's worth a visit. Even if it's only to sip sake and soak up the sights.

Yamashiro
1999 N Sycamore Ave., Los Angeles 90068
yamashirohollywood.com

Neighborhood: Hollywood
Kid friendly status up to you, parents.

RAISE A GLASS
TO L.A.'S CRAFT BREWERIES AND DISTILLERIES

Over the past several years, L.A. has been flooded with new craft breweries and distilleries, and curious imbibers should make a point to explore the burgeoning scene. In fact, until less than a decade ago L.A. hadn't seen any new small-scale producers since before Prohibition, and now there are around 60 craft breweries and about a half dozen distilleries across the county with more opening all the time. Because we don't have room for them all, we've highlighted a few of our favorites.

To discover more, check out the Los Angeles County Brewers Guild (labrewersguild.org) and the California Artisanal Distillers Guild (cadistillers.org).

Neighborhood: All of Los Angeles
Adults only (except where kids are allowed)

Craft Breweries

Eagle Rock Brewery
(eaglerockbrewery.com)
3056 Rosewell St., Los Angeles 90065

MacLeod Ale Brewing Co.
(macleodale.com)
14741 Calvert St., Van Nuys 91411

Dry River Brewing
(dryriverbrewing.com)
671 S Anderson St., Los Angeles 90023

Ladyface Ale Companie
(ladyfaceale.com)
29281 Agoura Rd., Agoura Hills

Monkish Brewing Company
(monkishbrewing.com)
20311 S Western Ave., Torrance 90501

Angel City Brewery
(angelcitybrewery.com)
216 Alameda St., Los Angeles 90012

Craft Distilleries

Greenbar Distillery
(greenbardistillery.com)
2459 E 8th St., Los Angeles 90021

The Spirit Guild
(thespiritguild.com)
586 Mateo St., Los Angeles 90013

Stark Spirits Distillery
(starkspirits.com)
1260 Lincoln Ave. #1100, Pasadena 91103

R6 Distilling
(r6distillery.com)
909 E El Segundo Blvd., El Segundo 90245

PICK PRODUCE WITH CELEBRITY CHEFS
AT FARMERS' MARKETS

L.A. offers an embarrassment of riches when it comes to locally grown, organic produce piled high at farmers' markets across the city. As a bonus, there's a good chance you'll rub elbows with a celebrity chef while you're both reaching for that beautiful heirloom tomato. Many of the top chefs in town head to the farmers' markets to personally pick out the choicest seasonal ingredients for that night's menu. If you strike up a conversation, one of those chefs may just let you in on a cooking tip or let you know which farmer has the best goods. One of the best places for a possible celeb chef sighting is the Santa Monica Farmers' Market held on Wednesdays, one of the biggest and best in the country—though you might also try the sprawling Hollywood Farmers' Market on Sundays.

Neighborhood: All over Los Angeles
Kid friendly

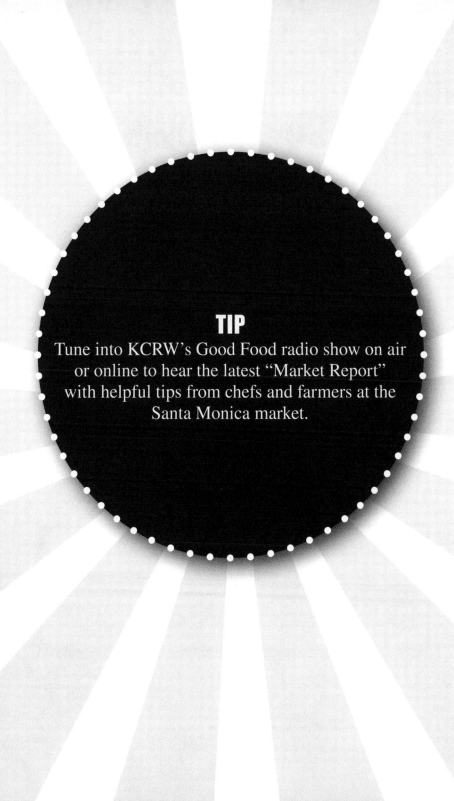

TIP
Tune into KCRW's Good Food radio show on air or online to hear the latest "Market Report" with helpful tips from chefs and farmers at the Santa Monica market.

DOUBLE DOWN
AT IN-N-OUT

Do not snub this fast-food chain—we're talking about a SoCal institution here, not McDonald's. Order a classic Double-Double with Animal Style fries and find out why locals and out-of-towners jones for In-N-Out more than a morning caffeine fix. Need an even stronger endorsement to keep from driving by? Anthony Bourdain admitted that it's one of his favorite restaurants in L.A. and makes a point to stop for a Double-Double Animal Style when he first arrives in town (and usually again before he leaves.)

LAX location:
9149 S Sepulveda Blvd., Los Angeles 90045
in-n-out.com

Neighborhood: All over Los Angeles
Kid friendly

TIP
The In-N-Out near LAX is the perfect place to get your fix immediately upon arrival or as your last chance before you leave. You can even hitch a ride from the terminal on the Sepulveda Parking Spot courtesy shuttle for free if you're desperate, 'cause In-N-Out is located right next-door.

FORAGE FOR FRUIT
IN THE NEIGHBORHOOD

Thanks to our wonderful Mediterranean climate in L.A., a bounty of delicious produce can be found growing all around us practically year-round, often temptingly hanging from our neighbors' trees. But rather than let those ripe avocados and citrus fruits go to waste, you can legally pick produce from branches that hang into public space. The Fallen Fruit art collective has created helpful maps of L.A. that show where that produce is waiting to be foraged (though it's recommended that you ask the owner first if you see them).

You can also volunteer with Food Forward, which rescues surplus produce from farms, farmers' markets, and wholesale markets, then donates it all to hunger relief organizations. Or you might want to join writer and naturalist Pascal Bauder for one of his Urban Outdoor Skills classes, which include making wild beers or finding culinary and medicinal herbs from foraged ingredients.

Fallen Fruit
fallenfruit.org

Food Forward
foodforward.org

Urban Outdoor Skills
urbanoutdoorskills.com

Neighborhood: All over Los Angeles
Kid friendly status up to you, parents.

FIND REFUGE
AT THE ROOSEVELT HOTEL

Old, glamorous—and possibly haunted—if you can stay at The Roosevelt while you're in town, that's a list topper all on its own. However, if you're stuck inside the Hollywood/Highland tourist trap, it's the perfect place to seek refuge. After indulging a friend's quest to obtain a "Map to the Stars" or watching them compare their feet to Fred Astaire's concrete footprints across the street at the Chinese Theatre, you can pop in to The Roosevelt afterwards to catch your breath. Have a seat in the grandiose hotel lobby and soak up all that Spanish-style opulence—or even better—meander outside and make your way to the poolside bar. Once you're sipping an alcoholic Orange Julius and gazing up at the palm trees that perfectly frame the old historic exterior, you'll have yourself a real L.A. moment. And if you care for a bit of vintage bowling with your cocktail, head up to The Spare Room bar for a few frames.

7000 Hollywood Blvd., Los Angeles 90028
hehollywoodroosevelt.com

Neighborhood: Hollywood
Kid friendly

FUN FACTS

The Hollywood Roosevelt opened in 1927 and housed the 1st Academy Awards show in 1929. Clark Gable, Charlie Chaplin, Shirley Temple, and Marilyn Monroe are just a few on the roster of famous guests. Iconic '60s pop artist David Hockney hand painted the tiles in the swimming pool!

SOAR BACK IN TIME
ABOARD A PAN AM FLIGHT

Revel in the style and class of the Golden Age of air travel without ever leaving the ground. The Pan Am Experience offers the chance to climb aboard an exact replica of the pioneering airline's Boeing 747 with a double-decker cabin that's been painstakingly restored down to the last retro detail. Sip cocktails from the open bar while Sinatra croons overhead, order up a Chateaubriand steak carved seat-side as part of a 5-course meal, shop vintage perfumes from the duty-free cart, and enjoy a fashion show of the iconic uniforms of Pan Am flight attendants. The attention to detail is impressive and makes for a one-of-a-kind experience, even if it is a bit of a splurge. Trust us, you'll miss the pampering the next time you fly for real.

The Pan Am Experience
13240 Weidner St., Pacoima 91331
panamexperience.com

Neighborhood: San Fernando Valley
Adults only

TIP

Be sure to allow extra time after the experience for an included tour of the Air Hollywood studios where the aircraft interior and airport scenes for practically every TV show, movie, and commercial are filmed. Air Hollywood also offers classes to help people overcome their fear of flying, and there is a free program to help children with autism and developmental disabilities get comfortable with air travel.

GRAB A LATE-NIGHT BREAKFAST
AT THE ORIGINAL PANTRY

The owners of The Original Pantry say they have never locked the doors of their café, nor have they ever been without a customer since 1924, so it's a prime spot to absorb a bit of L.A.'s history. While it's more about the charm and less about the food at The Original Pantry, after you've enjoyed some late-night French Toast at 1:00 am, you can check another L.A. rite of passage off your list. Lines get long during the day, but don't get discouraged—things move pretty fast. It's also one of the few places in Downtown L.A. with a large (and cheap!) parking lot. Bring cash and expect large portions.

877 S Figueroa St., Los Angeles 90017
pantrycafe.com

Neighborhood: Downtown
Kid friendly

FIND THE SECRET ENTRANCES
TO STYLISH SPEAKEASIES

While we thankfully no longer have Prohibition laws forcing our favorite watering holes underground, there's still plenty of allure to covertly grabbing a drink in a speakeasy-style bar. In recent years, plenty of secret cocktail hideaways have quietly opened where knowing a password or finding a hidden entrance grants you access to an intricately designed interior with great drinks. From intimate, dimly lit cocktail sanctuaries to rollicking retro-themed bars, on the following pages are some of our favorites (with tips on how to get in).

The Varnish (Downtown)
One of the first to kick off the recent speakeasy boom.
Once you enjoy a French Dip at Cole's, consider heading
to the unmarked door at the back.

Good Times at Davey Wayne's (Hollywood)
To make your way into this swingin' '70s themed love
shack, look for a retro garage sale in an alleyway and
go for a cold one through the refrigerator.

The Walker Inn (Koreatown)
While the cocktails are excellent at The Normandie Club,
there's a little buzzer in the back of the bar which lets
you into a secret spot for even more elaborate drinks
(or you can make a reservation online).

Blind Barber (Culver City)
Make your way to the back of the barbershop
(unless you need a quick trim first) and look for the
unmarked door.

Old Lightning (Venice)
If you're a fan of rare liquors and classic cocktails,
ask your server at Scopa Italian Roots about where to go,
or you can make a reservation online.

The Exhibition Room (Long Beach)
Get the secret password by making a reservation online,
and then head to the 1940s-era phone booth in the back
to discover a Prohibition-themed bar with live music,
burlesque, and more.

Neighborhood: All over Los Angeles
Adults only

KICK BACK
IN K-TOWN

K-Town, a.k.a. Koreatown, is a place to flock to for three big reasons: the spas, the BBQ, and the karaoke.

Korean spas are unlike most of the tranquil, pampering, happy places most of us know and love, but all kinds of women go nuts over the scrubs, which are definitely the main attraction. Calling the rubdown vigorous is an understatement, and oh yeah—you're completely in the buff, too. But if you can let your inhibitions go, the reward is walking out relaxed with skin softer than the day you were born. Try Olympic or Natura Spa.

Olympic Spa, 3915 W Olympic Blvd., Los Angeles 90019
olympicspala.com

Natura Spa, 3240 Wilshire Blvd., Los Angeles 90010
natura-spa.com

Adults only

As for the BBQ, it only takes one visit and you'll be singing the praises of the outrageously delicious marinated meat like everyone else. Enhance the social experience and choose a spot where the grilling is left up to you. Korean restaurants are known for the small grills in the middle of the table to cook the meat, and many offer all-you-can-eat options as well. (Don't worry, you don't have to DIY if cooking isn't your thing). Newbies, don't be intimidated by all the banchan (side dishes that complement the meal) on the table—the offerings may look unfamiliar to some Westerners, but put yourself out there and you can discover the goodness of kimchi and more! Chosun Galbee is a great place to start.

Chosun Galbee, 3330 W Olympic Blvd., Los Angeles 90019
chosungalbee.com
Kid friendly

Top off your meal with an after-party at one of the many karaoke establishments in K-town to make your night truly legendary. Whether you're rolling two or twenty people deep, a private room awaits you so you can belt out your favorite songs without getting stage fright. After all the soju you probably drank at dinner, this is a great place to get rowdy without annoying others, and the food and drinks can continue flowing while you sing karaoke all night. Star Karaoke is usually a reliable option.

Star Karaoke, 601 S Ardmore Ave., Los Angeles 90005
facebook.com/thestarkaraoke/
Adults only

NOSH
AT CANTER'S DELI

Open 24 hours with great people-watching opportunities around the clock, Canter's is an L.A. icon where countless rock and movie stars have dined since opening in 1931. The Matzo Ball Soup is as comforting as a hug from your mother. And while Langer's Deli may be L.A.'s reigning champ for pastrami sandwiches, the one at Canter's is very respectable. Get your fill of the bagel chips and pickles before your food arrives, while admiring the retro chic décor. Canter's isn't trying to be hip; it's just timelessly cool.

Also, be sure to stop by the bakery counter to have some chocolate chip rugelach boxed up to go.

419 N Fairfax Ave.
Los Angeles 90036
cantersdeli.com

Neighborhood:
Miracle Mile/Mid-City
Kid friendly

TIP
Grownups should stop by the Kibitz Room,
Canter's adjoining cocktail lounge for music and comedy.
It's been a popular hangout for rock legends from Joni Mitchell and
The Doors to Guns N' Roses and the latest indie bands.

SCREAM FOR
(WEIRD) ICE CREAM!

Chocolate chip and cookies 'n' cream just doesn't cut it in L.A. anymore—challenge yourself and go on a weird ice cream flavor quest. Mashti Malone's in Hollywood has been serving up flavors like Rosewater Saffron with Pistachios since 1980, proving that unusual ice cream isn't just a fad. If you're more of a Fried Chicken and Waffle ice cream kind of person, go to Coolhaus in Culver City, and be sure to choose the Potato Chip and Skor cookies to make it an ice cream sandwich. You can even offer suggestions of your own for flavors at Scoops on the Westside or at the original location in East Hollywood; although they aren't always executed, somehow Goat Cheese Lavender ice cream made the cut, so you've got a fighting chance. And Wanderlust Creamery in Atwater Village and Tarzana scoops up creative, internationally inspired flavors like Sticky Rice and Mango, Ube Malted Crunch, and Pretzel with Rúgbrauð (Icelandic rye bread).

Mashti Malone's Ice Cream
1525 N La Brea Ave.
Los Angeles 90028
mashtimalone.com

Scoops
3400 Overland Ave.
Los Angeles 90034
scoopswestside.com

Coolhaus
8588 W Washington Blvd.
Culver City 90232
eatcoolhaus.com

Wanderlust Creamery
3134 Glendale Blvd.
Los Angeles 90039
wanderlustcreamery.com

SIP WINE
WHERE THE WILD THINGS ARE

As much as you might enjoy wine, you've never fully appreciated vino until you've sipped a glass in the company of wild animals. Thanks to Malibu Wine Safaris, you can finally get to that level of appreciation. Hop aboard an open-air jeep to explore the 1,000 Acre Saddlerock Ranch and vineyards of Malibu wines, where you can meet, feed, and take a selfie with camels, zebras, alpacas, bison, and, of course, Stanley the Giraffe. Along the way, you'll sample six different wines at two separate tastings, which will no doubt also help increase your appreciation of the animals. It's a wild experience you likely won't find anywhere else.

Malibu Wines also offers sailing excursions with tastings and has live music at its tasting room on Saturdays and Sundays.

Malibu Wine Safari
32111 Mullholland Hwy., Malibu 90265
lasafaris.com/#home

Neighborhood: Malibu
Adults only

FIND AMAZING MEXICAN FOOD
IN BOYLE HEIGHTS

Although a Mexican restaurant is practically a stone's throw away from any given location in L.A., Boyle Heights is where some of the best options are.

For old-school home-style dishes, head to Casa Fina Restaurant & Cantina, and for a burrito as big as your forearm, it's all about Manuel's Original El Tepeyac Café, and for one stuffed with a chile relleno, head to the legendary Al & Bea's. Keep Puertos del Pacifico in mind for seafood (and $1 Taco Tuesdays!), or try more fantastic tacos at Guisados or Los Cinco Puntos. Drop by La Mascota Bakery to bring home a few goodies for dessert and consider the night a success.

Neighborhood: East Los Angeles
Kid friendly

TIP
Be sure to spend some time at Mariachi Plaza, the historic square where mariachi bands play to get gigs at weddings, birthdays, anniversary parties, and quinceañeras (celebration of a girl's 15th birthday).

DRINK
AND DON'T DRIVE
WITH THE METRO

L.A.'s sprawling city limits can really cramp your style, especially if you're planning to partake in the nightlife. Even though L.A.'s Metro is the second largest public transportation system in the U.S. (after New York's MTA), many forget that Metro can help you get to where you're going without having to worry about the drive. Operating up to around 2 am on Friday and Saturday nights, you can enjoy the night—right up to last call. It's also cheaper than ride-sharing services and is more of an adventure.

If you start in Downtown and use Union Station as your hub, you can:

- Take the Gold Line—Gets you to Little Tokyo after one stop, and you're just one block from Far Bar. Or, take it in the opposite direction to get to Old Town Pasadena for a beer at Kings Row or a drink at the divey Freddie's 35er.
- Take the Red Line—Head right to the Hollywood/Vine stop to hit up the infamous Frolic Room or cocktails at Lost Property Bar.
- Take the Purple Line—Direct route to Koreatown, where soju shots and karaoke await. Get the party started at The Prince and figure out what's next from there.
- Take the Expo Line—You'll need to transfer to this line by taking either the Red or Purple Line to the 7th St/Metro Center stop. Once on the Expo, you can take it all the way to downtown Santa Monica and grab a craft beer at West 4th and Jane or a stiff drink and live music at Harvelle's.

Neighborhood: All over Los Angeles
Adults only

SAVOR "TEA BY THE SEA"
AT THE GETTY VILLA

It may sound like an afternoon for the upper crust of the bourgeoisie, but really, it's an excuse to sip tea and sample the herbs and vegetables that are authentically grown in the Villa's re-created 1st century Roman garden. As you gaze out from the floor-to-ceiling windows, let your eyes feast on the gorgeous grounds while you feast on freshly baked tea breads and scones. It's a surefire way to elevate an already heightened experience; The Getty Villa is indisputably one of the most breathtaking campuses in L.A. Also, check The Getty's schedule for garden tours, guest lectures, and performances in the outdoor amphitheater.

17985 Pacific Coast Hwy., Pacific Palisades 90272
getty.edu

Neighborhood: Pacific Palisades
Kid friendly
Thursdays & Saturdays at 1:00pm

DINE IN SECRET
AT UNDERGROUND SUPPER CLUBS

Drinking in speakeasy-style bars isn't the only thing we like to do in secret in L.A. We also enjoy stealing away to underground supper clubs for a clandestine dinner date. While many of these underground dinner parties can be difficult to track down and often require knowing someone on the inside, others require only a bit of sleuthing. These dinners often take place in unique locations and feature wildly creative dishes you won't find elsewhere, and you'll often wind up making new friends with your fellow adventurous food lovers. In most cases you need to sign up for their newsletter to find out when the next dinner will be.

Disco Dining Club
discodiningclub.com

The Coconut Club
thecoconutclubla.com

Wolvesmouth
wolvesmouth.com/mailing-list

Re Creo Supper Club
recreosupperclub.com/locations-1-1/

Food Shop
lafoodshop.com

Place Invaders
placeinvaders.com/users/sign_in

Because The Wind
becausethewind.com

Neighborhood: All over Los Angeles
Adults only, mostly

DEVOUR SOME
DIM SUM

A champagne breakfast brunch is all fine and good, but real foodies in L.A. ditch the mimosas for the dim sum cart. With such a huge Asian population (and the even bigger influence that population has on L.A. culture), dim sum is a mandatory experience. Be prepared to wait in line and deal with crowds, but once those delectable dumplings arrive at your table, you'll understand the hype.

Undisputed top honors go to Sea Harbour in Rosemead, but for more of the best of the best, check out other San Gabriel Valley favorites like Lunasia, Elite, or China Red. Beginners, start with har gow (shrimp dumplings) and shao mai (pork dumplings) and you'll work your way up to the fung zau (chicken feet) like a pro in no time.

Sea Harbour Seafood Restaurant
3939 Rosemead Blvd., Rosemead 91770
(626) 288-3939

Neighborhood: San Gabriel Valley
Kid friendly

BUY A ROUND WITH A VIEW
AT A ROOFTOP BAR

There's something about sipping a cocktail on a rooftop that makes the drink taste (and the views look) that much better. Lucky for us, we've got plenty of excellent options to imbibe with some altitude. Here are some of our *top* picks:

Neighborhood: All over Los Angeles
Adults only

Upstairs at Ace Hotel (Downtown)
Gothic spires, desert chic designs, and killer cocktails.
929 S Broadway, Los Angeles 90015
acehotel.com/losangeles/upstairs

E.P. & L.P. (West Hollywood)
Views of the Hollywood Hills, great drinks,
and incredible food.
603 La Cienega Blvd., West Hollywood 90069
eplosangeles.com

Broken Shaker at the Freehand Hotel (Downtown)
Tropical cocktails, colorful pool parties,
and plenty of style.
416 W 8th St., Los Angeles 90014
freehandhotels.com/los-angeles/broken-shaker/

Spire 73 at the InterContinental Hotel (Downtown)
The tallest open-air bar in the Western Hemisphere.
900 Wilshire Blvd., Los Angeles 90017
dtla.intercontinental.com/dining/

High Rooftop Lounge at Hotel Erwin (Venice)
Beach views, ocean breezes, and DJs.
1697 Pacific Ave., Venice 90291
hotelerwin.com/high-rooftop-lounge

Mama Shelter (Hollywood)
Heart of Hollywood, colorful furniture,
games, and great eats.
6500 Selma Ave., Los Angeles 90028
mamashelter.com/en/los-angeles

WATCH THE SUNSET
AT NELSON'S

If you're staying at the Terranea Resort, you've definitely accomplished something bucket list–worthy already. The sprawling property perched high on the cliffs of Palos Verdes is magical all on its own. Facing the Pacific Ocean and boasting views out to Catalina Island, it's quickly become the crown jewel of the entire South Bay. But the on-site restaurant, Nelson's, offers something a little more accessible—all you have to do is park yourself by the fire pit and enjoy one of the most drop-dead gorgeous sunsets you've ever seen in your life. Return often and repeat; this is worth doing any chance you can get.

Nelson's at Terranea
100 Terranea Way, Rancho Palos Verdes 90275
terranea.com

Neighborhood: South Bay
Kid friendly status is all up to you, parents.

TIP
Another great oceanfront option for watching the sunset is Duke's in Malibu, especially if you stop by on Fridays at 4 pm for Aloha Hour with discounted Mai Tais and Hawaiian dancers.
21150 Pacific Coast Hwy., Malibu 90265
dukesmalibu.com

TASTE VINO
FROM L.A.'S LAST PRODUCING WINERY

Long before all the concrete, freeways, and skyscrapers were even imagined in Downtown L.A., San Antonio Winery had flourishing vineyards. After the Depression and Prohibition shut down most of its competitors, San Antonio managed to stay alive by producing sacramental wines and, even after much of the business moved up north (to what's now known as Wine Country), the winery stayed loyal to Los Angeles. Though the vineyards are gone today, the historic winery still stands and is open seven days a week for tasting, shopping, or dining. The tastings each include four wines, and they range in scope and price from the Traditional selection ($10) to the Artisan Premiere ($25) and include a guided tour. The grapes used today are from the winery's vineyards in Monterey, but if you want to split hairs, the bottling and distributing are still done in L.A., so San Antonio is still technically the last producing winery in town.

737 Lamar St., Los Angeles 90031
sanantoniowinery.com

Neighborhood: Downtown
Kid friendly (except for the drinking, of course)

LINE DANCE
AT THE LAST HONKY TONK BAR IN L.A.

While most people don't associate Los Angeles with cowboys—
except maybe on a soundstage—you can still find the charm of
the Old West preserved at The Cowboy Palace Saloon. Tucked in
the northwest corner of the San Fernando Valley, this beloved bar
has been a local favorite for decades and remains a hidden gem.

Saunter through the swinging doors, order a drink at the bar
beneath a hanging display of worn-out cowboy boots, and get
ready for a night of line dancing and live country music. You'll
likely recognize the classic country look of the bar from cameos
in countless TV shows, movies, and music videos, including
Toby Keith's "I Love This Bar." Don't worry if you've never
line danced before; they offer free dance lessons nightly, and the
friendly crowd couldn't be more welcoming. Check the calendar
for the class schedule and band lineups.

The Cowboy Palace Saloon
21635 Devonshire St., Chatsworth 91311
thecowboypalacesaloon.com

Neighborhood: San Fernando Valley
Adults only

PARTY LIKE A CELEBRITY
AT CHATEAU MARMONT

Chateau Marmont = celebrity. Period. Famous people come to stay, play, work, and party, at this legendary Hollywood apartment house built in the late '20s. Even though many creatives have holed up here to write scripts, and even more actors have checked in when working in town, not all guests have to be famous. If you're going to kick down and book a room, just keep your cool and be respectful. As famous as the Chateau is, it's not for lookie-loos; so don't cruise in toting an SLR camera around your neck and definitely ditch the tabloids when you're squeezing in some poolside reading. If you can't pay to stay, fake it and party at the bar.

8221 Sunset Blvd., Los Angeles 90046
chateaumarmont.com

Neighborhood: West Hollywood
Not so kid friendly

CHICKEN DANCE
AT ALPINE VILLAGE

Don your finest lederhosen and dirndl (or whatever's comfortable for dancing and drinking) and head to the historic Alpine Village in Torrance for a Bavarian bash. Known for its epic Oktoberfest celebrations since 1968, this German-themed village is open year-round and merits a visit (it's also less crowded during the off-season). There you'll find a restaurant serving up hearty German fare (Schnitzel! Bratwurst! Spätzle!) and steins full of Bavarian brews. You can also catch Oom Pah Pah bands, learn to chicken dance, and meander the streets of the re-created village shopping for artisanal German crafts, baked goodies, sausages, beer, and more to take home.

Alpine Village
833 W Torrance Blvd., Torrance 90502
alpinevillagecenter.com

Neighborhood: Torrance
Kid friendly (except for the drinking portion, of course)

ORDER A POST-MIDNIGHT BASEBALL STEAK
AT PACIFIC DINING CAR

Since 1921—two years before the Hollywood (land) sign went up—the Pacific Dining Car has been a beloved treasure for Angelenos looking to enjoy an excellent steak and other classic American fare, even into the wee hours of the night. Styled with the elegance of a vintage train car, full of dark woods and rich tones of green, red and blue, the under-the-radar hideaway is the only 24-hour fine dining restaurant in the city, offering an unsurpassed option for revelers or anyone fixing for an after-hours bite. Sure, it's a pricier than a taco truck, but the late-night menu (available 10pm to 6am) offers more accessible prices for many of its classic dishes such as the signature baseball steak, a juicy 10-ounce top sirloin end cut—immortalized in the movie Training Day—which goes for $24 late-night, about half the usual price. After midnight, you're also likely to witness an incredible cross-section of L.A., including Hollywood producers, off-duty cops, and plenty of mysterious characters enjoying the hushed tones and plush booths.

1310 W 6th St., Los Angeles 90017 (Original location)
2700 Wilshire Blvd., Santa Monica 90403
pacificdiningcar.com

Neighborhood: Westlake and Santa Monica
Kid friendly status is all up to you, parents.

ART AND ENTERTAINMENT

36

EXPLORE
WONDERFULLY WEIRD MUSEUMS

Los Angeles offers plenty of fantastic traditional museums to explore, but there's no shortage of other unique, and sometimes wacky, cultural institutions that are also worth investigating. Here are some of our favorites:

Museum of Jurassic Technology (Culver City)
Before you Google "Jurassic Technology," please just stop. This place is one that's better gone into with no prior expectations. It's more "Odditorium" than Louvre.

Velveteria (Chinatown)
Maybe you've seen velvet paintings in a dorm room or dive bar, but there's nothing quite like this impressive collection showcasing more than 450 of the owners' 3,000 quirky paintings.

Museum of Death (Hollywood)
For those with a morbid curiosity (and who are not faint of heart) this macabre museum showcases everything from crime scene photos and serial killer artwork to collections of coffins and pet taxidermy.

The Bunny Museum (Altadena)

The "hoppiest" place on earth features more than 34,000 bunny-themed artifacts inside a bunny-loving couple's home. And yes, real bunnies to pet as well.

Holyland Exhibition (Silver Lake)

Considered to be the real-life inspiration for Indiana Jones, Antonia F. Futternutter amassed an enormous collection of artifacts from the Middle East beginning in the 1920s. From 5,000-year-old oil lamps and jewelry to a 2,700-year-old sarcophagus, there's plenty to marvel at during the guided, by-appointment-only tours.

Neighborhood: All over Los Angeles
Kid friendly status is all up to you, parents.

37

EXPERIENCE CINEMA'S GOLDEN AGE
AT HISTORIC MOVIE PALACES

Here in the movie capital of the world, where you watch movies is often as important as what you watch. And while attending a screening at a plush new multiplex can be great, nothing rivals watching a classic film in one of L.A.'s grand old movie palaces.

Several of the most famous theaters can be found right in the heart of Hollywood and were developed in the 1920s by legendary showman Sid Grauman and Charles Toberman, who was often called "The Father of Hollywood." There's the Chinese Theatre with its famous forecourt of celebrity handprints and footprints in the cement pavement blocks out front, and the Egyptian Theatre with its towering columns and hieroglyphs. And at the impressive El Capitan, which once showcased the world premiere of *Citizen Kane* and is now owned by Disney, you can catch a live pre-movie stage performance by Disney characters with organ music.

Downtown, spectacular vintage theaters are found along Broadway, home to the largest concentration of movie palaces left in the U.S. While some have been converted to retail use, many are still used for screenings thanks to programs like Cinespia (at historical locations throughout the area) and the L.A. Conservancy's Last Remaining Seats. Notables include Grauman's Million Dollar Theater, the Los Angeles Theatre, and the Palace Theatre. The United Artists Theatre, originally opened by Charlie Chaplin, Mary Pickford, Douglas Fairbanks, and D.W. Griffith, is now known as The Theatre at Ace Hotel, featuring special movie nights as well as live music and other special events.

Neighborhood: All over Los Angeles
Kid friendly

CRUISE THE
NEON JUNGLE

Hop on a double-decker bus and "ooh" and "aah" over the bright (neon) lights of the city. Most Saturday nights from June to September, the Museum of Neon Art in Glendale leads Neon Cruises, bus tours that showcase the coolest neon signs and the most obscure neon artwork that can be found throughout the city. The museum also occasionally hosts special tours throughout the year, including a Holiday Lights Cruise, a Valentine's Day Cruise, and a Neon Noir Cruise. Let the pros at MONA help you see the light—a neon bus tour in L.A. is something you just must do. You should also definitely visit the museum to get an up-close look at spectacular neon art that once lit up the night in L.A. and beyond.

Museum of Neon Art
216 S Brand Blvd., Glendale 91204
neonmona.org

Neighborhood: All over Los Angeles
Adults only (for the tours)

WATCH MARTY AND ELAYNE
IN ACTION

If you've seen the movie *Swingers*, you were lucky enough to catch a glimpse of Marty and Elayne's act at The Dresden. Don't settle for just a cameo; seeing Marty and Elayne is believing. The endearing duo has been doing their thing for 30 years, and they still appear in the Lounge on Tuesday through Saturday nights from 9:00 pm to 1:15 am. Since the movie is such a revered guide to L.A. on its own, you know Marty and Elayne are legit, so go ahead and boost your hipster credentials and catch something special before it's gone.

Afraid of hipsters? Go to The Dresden anyway. The 60-year-old Hollywood restaurant and lounge delivers an authentic Rat Pack kind of vibe, and certainly one that's unmistakably L.A.

The Dresden
1760 N Vermont Ave., Los Angeles 90027
thedresden.com

Neighborhood: Hollywood
Adults only

BE DAZZLED
BY DIY ART HOUSES

Museums and art galleries aren't the only places where you'll find spectacular works of art in L.A. Throughout the city, Angelenos have created incredible sculptures right on their front lawns. Often created using everyday household items and found objects, these works of art turn the ordinary into the extraordinary. (Just remember that most of these are private residences, so be respectful, and don't disturb the occupants unless they invite you in.)

Randyland's *Phantasma Gloria* (Echo Park)

The centerpiece of Randyland, a sculpture garden created by artist Randlette Lawrence, is the massive *Phantasma Gloria* sculpture that can be seen from the street. The solar mosaic, called a "sky catcher," is a dazzling 50-foot-long, 24-foot-tall sculpture of the Virgin of Guadalupe made with steel rebar and blown glass vessels filled with colored water that reflect sunlight. Try contacting Randlette via his Facebook Page to schedule a visit.

1648 Lemoyne St., Los Angeles 90026
facebook.com/RandylandLA/

The Chandelier Tree (Silver Lake)

This popular date destination features a huge tree with 30 vintage chandeliers hung from its branches to create one of the most magical effects you'll catch in L.A. at night. Started as just an experiment, the artist Adam Tenenbaum (who lives in the house) hung a few of the chandeliers in the tree after finding that they were too large to be indoors. He kept acquiring more, and this heartwarming local spectacle was born.

2811 W Silver Lake Dr., Los Angeles 90039
chandeliertree.com

The Mosaic Tile House (Venice)

Tucked on a quiet residential street, The Mosaic Tile House is the work of married artists Cheri Pann and Gonzalo Duran, and nearly every square inch of the house—both inside and out—is covered in stunningly colorful ceramic tile fragments. They regularly host tours, so be sure to check their website for the schedule.

1116 Palms Blvd., Los Angeles 90291
cheripann.com/The_Mosaic_Tile_House.html

Neighborhood: All over Los Angeles
Kid friendly

41

HANG OUT
WITH THE BOB BAKER MARIONETTES

Performances like the ones at the Bob Baker Marionette Theater simply don't exist today in our world of Nick Jr. heavyweights and Disney Channel superstars. Enjoy this sweet slice of nostalgia complete with a cup of ice cream that's served right after the show! Almost any local has fond childhood memories of the Bob Baker Marionettes, and it's those warm fuzzies that keep audiences coming back with each new generation. Help keep it alive.

1345 W 1st St., Los Angeles 90026
bobbakermarionettetheater.com

Neighborhood: Silver Lake
Kid friendly

CATCH A FLICK
AT THE HOLLYWOOD FOREVER CEMETERY

Catching a film outdoors at The Hollywood Forever Cemetery is one of the most unique experiences you can have in L.A. Don't worry, you won't be camping out on anyone's final resting place. Out on the lawn, with the ornate headstones behind you and the stars above, the screenings bring new meaning to cinema as a spiritual experience.

Cinespia shows films at historical locations throughout the year, including downtown's vintage movie palaces, but the series at the cemetery is hugely popular. Don't play cool and arrive fashionably late—with 4,000 moviegoers at most screenings, you gotta line up early to stake out a spot. You also want time to explore the grounds; some of the famous grave markers and mausoleums date back to 1899.

Pack a picnic dinner and bring blankets to sit on. DJs play before and after, and there's an elaborate photo booth inspired by the night's film. Buy tickets online and pony up for on-site parking to avoid schlepping your stuff in from outside the gates.

6000 Santa Monica Blvd.
Los Angeles 90038
cinespia.org

Neighborhood: Hollywood
Adults only
Seasonal: May through September

TIP
Snap an obligatory shot of Johnny Ramone's rock 'n' roll resting place to earn bragging rights on social media.

ADMIRE THE DEDICATION
BEHIND THE WATTS TOWERS

Watts can be a rough part of town, but checking out these idyllic mosaic structures is a great opportunity to learn more about the neighborhood. When you learn that these towers were designed and built by just one man over the course of 33 years, the history becomes as intriguing as the spectacle. You don't really need to take a guided tour; you can just pop by and walk around the gated towers yourself for free. Allow enough time to admire from afar and be sure to peer through the gates for a closer look—the towers are decorated with found objects, so it's a perfect opportunity to squeeze in a little game of "I Spy" with the kiddos. If you want more, 30-minute guided tours are available Thursdays through Saturdays, 10:30 am to 3:00 pm and Sundays 12:30 to 3:00 pm.

Watts Towers
1727 E 107th St., Los Angeles 90002
wattstowers.us

Neighborhood: South LA
Kid friendly

TIP

While you're in the neighborhood, stop by the Watts Coffee House. It's been a community hub for years, carrying on the tradition of the original Watts Happening Coffee House that opened after the Watts Riots in 1965. Enjoy fried chicken and waffles or a breakfast plate with eggs, grits, and biscuits, and be sure to explore the memorabilia and photos on the wall celebrating African American icons, culture, and history.

Watts Coffee House
1827 E 103rd St., Los Angeles 90002
facebook.com/whereweprepareourfoodwith-LOVE/

MAKE YOURSELF APPEAR
AT THE MAGIC CASTLE

Once you flash your guest pass, prepare for a night of non-stop magic tricks along with dinner and drinks at this private club. You might not believe it, but a magic show at The Magic Castle really is one of the most exclusive invites you can score in Los Angeles.

Because of its exclusivity, there will be no spoilers in this book. Just know that they're not joking about the dress code, so dress sharp and keep it classy. You've gotta know the secret password or someone who does, so if you're lucky enough to score an invite, don't turn it down! The magic is cool, but this Victorian mansion nestled way up in the Hollywood Hills is quite the stunner too (with or without the hocus pocus).

7001 Franklin Ave., Los Angeles 90028
magiccastle.com

Neighborhood: Hollywood
Adults only

TIP
Having trouble getting on the guest list? Try visiting
The Magic Apple shop in Studio City and befriending a magician.
Or check The Magic Castle's schedule of performers and try reaching
out to one of the magicians via email or Facebook,
and if you're nice they may just offer passes.

LISTEN TO A FREE REHEARSAL
AT THE HOLLYWOOD BOWL

Summer in L.A. doesn't begin until The Bowl's season starts up. Performances range from classical concerts by the L.A. Philharmonic to rock shows with big name acts, as well as *Sound of Music* sing-a-longs and more fun. And for an extra special treat, you can be one of the lucky few to enjoy a free morning rehearsal.

Rehearsals are open to the public from early July until the middle of September on Tuesdays, Thursdays, and the occasional Wednesday, typically beginning at 9:30 am. Some Friday morning rehearsals for the summer's big headlining bands are open, too. Just be sure to call the box office before you go. Sit anywhere you like, including the coveted box seats as long as they aren't reserved for a special subscribers' event.

2301 N Highland Ave.	Neighborhood: Hollywood
Los Angeles 90068	Kid-friendly
hollywoodbowl.com	Seasonal

TIP
The Bowl is essentially a public park, operated by the county's Department of Parks and Recreation, so you can also explore the amphitheater walkways, plazas, and the Hollywood Bowl Museum for free.

STROLL THROUGH THE PAST
ON AN L.A. WALKING TOUR

They say nobody walks in L.A., but if it's with the L.A. Conservancy, you should help debunk that myth. The personal and passionate portrait captured by one of the organization's walking tours is just as fascinating for a local as for an out-of-town sightseer.

There's a strong architectural slant to each excursion (the Conservancy is an architectural and cultural preservation society after all), but history buffs and urban enthusiasts will find equal amounts of Los Angeles gold in each of the 12 different tours around downtown. Most tours last about 2.5 hours, and they span anywhere between the 19th century Victorian neighborhood of Angelino Heights or the theatres and retail spaces of days gone by on historic Broadway to the stunning and significant highlights of the modern skyline downtown.

laconservancy.org/tours

Neighborhood: Downtown
Not quite kid friendly, but special Family and Youth tours can be arranged.

GET ARTY
AT LACMA

Surprise—the Los Angeles County Museum of Art (LACMA) isn't just the biggest art museum on the West Coast; it's a cultural playground, too! For some of the really fun stuff, admission isn't even necessary. Plan to play a game of hide-and-seek inside Chris Burden's Urban Light, a stunning cluster of more than 200 restored lampposts and one of the most photographed sites in Los Angeles. Walk under, around, or beside Levitated Mass and debate whether a giant rock should be considered art or not. Sit in one of the swankiest modern outdoor lounges and order a few small plates and drinks from Ray's and Stark Bar. And if you do purchase tickets, don't skip Metropolis II, a miniature modern city that has 100,000 matchbox cars running through it.

5905 Wilshire Blvd., Los Angeles 90036
lacma.org

Neighborhood: Miracle Mile/Mid-City
Kid friendly

TIP
Be sure to check out LACMA's many cultural events held throughout the year such as free outdoor jazz nights on Fridays in the summer, curator talks, art classes, film screenings, and more.

ROCK OUT
AT AN ICONIC L.A. MUSIC VENUE

It's easy to catch a show in L.A. almost every night, but some venues are better than others (and certainly have more history!). If you find one of your favorite bands or musicians playing at one of these spots, you have no choice but to get tickets.

- **The El Rey** (Miracle Mile)—One of THE BEST small venues to see bands in L.A. The elegance of this theatre creates some killer ambiance to accompany the acts. No matter where you are, you're always pretty close to the stage.
- **The Greek** (Griffith Park)—A cozy outdoor amphitheater nestled in the hills, The Greek feels dreamy under the stars and much more intimate than the Hollywood Bowl.
- **The Troubadour** (West Hollywood)—So much music history in this place, it's mind-blowing; many legends have graced this stage, and many more have partied there themselves. Small club, standing room only. If Radiohead were playing (and they have!), you could catch a bottle of Thom Yorke's sweat from the stage while standing in the front row.
- **The Wiltern** (Koreatown)—A glorious green-tiled Art Deco theatre you can't miss on the corner of Wilshire/Western. A famous L.A. venue with massive credentials.

- **The Mint** (Mid-City)—This rollicking, intimate venue has hosted legendary performers since 1937, including Stevie Wonder, Natalie Cole, Ray Charles, and B.B. King, as well as more recent stars. Expect plenty of rock 'n' roll and roots music, and check out the old vinyl 45s covering the ceiling above the bar.
- **The Smell** (Downtown)—A bare bones, all-ages venue (no booze) for punk, indie rock, and experimental music. The current location is in danger of demolition, so go show your support.
- **McCabe's Guitar Shop** (Santa Monica)—Legendary musical instrument shop with a small stage in back that's been hosting notable folk acts since 1969.

Neighborhood: All over Los Angeles
Adults only (except for all-ages shows.)

ZOOM TO
LUCHA VAVOOM!

Go ahead and file this under the "totally out there" category; Lucha VaVOOM is a Mexican masked wrestling/burlesque/ comedy show that is not easily described or explained. Part WWF show, part circus with dashes of naughtiness, hilariousness, and the completely bizarre, you should probably just see it for yourself and draw your own conclusions. Famous fans include Jack Black (yep, that's where *Nacho Libre's* inspiration came from) and Fred Armisen. It's a pretty safe bet you'll end up with a story that starts out with, *"Remember that night we went to Lucha VaVOOM ..."*, so just take a leap of faith and investigate.

The Mayan Theater
1038 S Hill St., Los Angeles 90015
luchavavoom.com

Neighborhood: Downtown
Adults only

IMMERSE YOURSELF IN A MOVIE
AT THE CINERAMA DOME

With all the neon-lit megaplex theatres littering strip malls throughout SoCal, the iconic 1960s Cinerama Dome makes it a real occasion to go to the movies again. Perched right on Sunset Boulevard, the geodesic dome is one of Hollywood's most recognizable landmarks—and one of only three Cinerama theatres left in the U.S.

Grab your tub of popcorn and catch a flick on the Dome's 86-foot-wide screen and see what the rare three-projector Cinerama process is all about. In response to threats of demolition, L.A. preservationists fought to keep the historic dome intact, so not only will you have your unique experience, but you'll also help to keep the experience alive for future moviegoers to enjoy.

6360 Sunset Blvd., Los Angeles 90028
arclightcinemas.com

Neighborhood: Hollywood
Kid friendly status is all up to you, parents.

BEAT THE HIGH SCORE
AT BUTTON MASH

For old-school pinball fanatics, video game nerds, and lovers of craft beer and creative eats, Button Mash is arcade heaven. The playfully designed bar-cade features well-maintained pinball machines, both vintage and new, as well as a huge selection of classic arcade games from the '80s and '90s like Galaga and Street Fighter II. They also have a great selection of craft beer and wine, plus tasty bites from pioneering underground supper club Starry Kitchen, including crispy tofu balls, a Korean pork belly sandwich, and dan dan noodles.

1391 Sunset Blvd., Los Angeles 90026
buttonmashla.com

Neighborhood: Echo Park
Kid friendly (until 9pm)

TIP
Button Mash is a great destination before or after a Dodgers game as the stadium is just up the road.

DISCOVER NEW ART
AT BERGAMOT STATION

Named for a wild flower and an old railroad station that was abandoned decades ago, Bergamot Station is now an excellent place to discover your new favorite artist. The sprawling campus-like complex features more than 40 galleries, mostly showcasing contemporary art. It's a great place to wander around and soak up tons of great art without having to trek all over to multiple galleries. Plus, they frequently have opening receptions and special events where you can meet the artists. There's also a small café with food and drinks, should you need a little pick-me-up between galleries.

Bergamot Station
2525 Michigan Ave., Santa Monica 90404

Neighborhood: Santa Monica
Kid friendly status up to you, parents.

TAKE A MURAL TOUR
OF WORLD-RENOWNED STREET ART

Los Angeles is home to hundreds of vibrantly colorful murals that reflect the city's rich culture, history, politics, and artistic spirit. The trick is knowing where to look for them. Once known as the "mural capital of the world"—thanks in large part to Chicano muralists of the 1960s and '70s and other artists—the proliferation of public art dropped off dramatically during an 11-year mural moratorium. Thanks to a recently passed ordinance, artists can now register their creations on a Murals Database, which has resulted in an increase in new murals and the preservation of historic ones. While you could certainly explore the city's murals on your own, mural tours hosted by the Mural Conservancy and L.A. Art Tours offer an up-close look at works created by local and international muralists, along with insight from a knowledgeable guide.

Mural Conservancy of Los Angeles
muralconservancy.org

L.A. Art Tours
laarttours.com

Neighborhood: Downtown
Kid friendly

TIP

Looking for more great street art?
Visit The Great Wall of Los Angeles,
an impressive half-mile mural in North
Hollywood that depicts the history of ethnic
groups in California from pre-history to the
present. It was painted by more than 400 kids and
their families over five summers beginning in
1974. sparcinla.org/programs/
the-great-wall-mural-los-angeles/

CAMP OUT BEFORE
THE ROSE PARADE

Get ready for a whole new take on a "Block Party"—camping out on Colorado Boulevard on the night before the Tournament of Roses Parade is one heck of a way to spend New Year's Eve. Not only will you secure a prime spot along the route, but you'll be participating in a long-standing tradition. Bring lawn chairs, blankets, sleeping bags, or anything else that will keep you cozy and prepare to not sleep all night (silly string and party hats optional). As you enjoy the view of all the floats passing by right in front of your eyes with all of the new friends you made the night before, you'll be glad that you partook in the festivities at least once.

Tournament of Roses Parade route
Colorado Blvd. (between Orange Grove Blvd. and Sierra Madre Blvd.)
tournamentofroses.com

Neighborhood: Pasadena
Kid friendly status is all up to you, parents.
Seasonal: The parade is held each year on New Year's Day
(except when it falls on a Sunday, then the parade is held on January 2)

TIP
If you can't hang all night, get up close and personal with the floats the day after the parade. The floats are on view for a limited time only on January 2. Check tournamentofroses.com for details.

PICNIC ON THE GRASS
AT THE GETTY CENTER

Wind your way up the hill on the museum's tram, step out onto the grounds, and prepare to be stupefied. Equally as beautiful as its sister campus at The Villa, The Getty Center is inspiring and majestic in a completely different way. You don't need to be an art enthusiast or architecture buff (although The Getty Center could be just the place to change your mind forever); just pack a picnic lunch (or grab a bite from the café) and find your own special spot on the grass to take it all in. If the expansive view over the city and the way the classical art is contrasted against the colossal modern architecture doesn't move you, it's unlikely that anything else in L.A. will.

1200 Getty Center Dr., Los Angeles 90049
getty.edu

Neighborhood: Brentwood
Kid friendly

TIP
The Getty Center frequently hosts musical performances, especially during the summer, so be sure to check the calendar before you go.

FORGET THE SCREEN
AND WATCH LIVE THEATER

While L.A. is deservedly known as a film and TV town, the city also offers a wide range of excellent theater to enjoy. In fact, many of the best actors and actresses you watch on screen hone their chops on stages around town. From classic productions on big stages to avant-garde productions in unexpected venues, here are some of our favorite theatre companies and venues that are well worth the price of admission:

Antaeus Theatre Company
antaeus.org

Sacred Fools
sacredfools.org

Deaf West Theatre Company
deafwest.org

REDCAT
redcat.org

A Noise Within
anoisewithin.org

The Los Angeles Theatre Center
thelatc.org

Independent Shakespeare Co.
iscla.org

The Theatre @ Boston Court
bostoncourt.com

Celebration Theatre
celebrationtheatre.com

BE A CONTESTANT
ON A GAME SHOW

It may be a little more difficult to play with Pat and Vanna than it used to be (most game shows today require potential contestants to audition), but there are two game shows left that you can get onto by just showing up. Anyone sitting in the studio audience at *The Price is Right* has a chance to *"Come on Down!"*, and if your costume's outrageous enough to catch Wayne Brady's eye, you could get chosen for *Let's Make a Deal.* Just reserve tickets to a taping of the show online; the tickets are free, you could be on TV, and you might win enough cash to pay for your kid's college—what's there to lose?

The Price is Right at CBS Television City Studios
7800 Beverly Blvd., Los Angeles 90036
on-camera-audiences.com/shows/The_Price_is_Right

Let's Make a Deal at Sunset Bronson Studios
5842 Sunset Blvd., Los Angeles 90028
on-camera-audiences.com/shows/Lets_Make_a_Deal

Neighborhood: Hollywood
Adults 18+

TIP
Camera shy? You can attend tapings of many other television shows in L.A. and enjoy watching others in the limelight. Visit tvtickets.com or Google your favorite show to see if you can sit in the studio audience.

SPORTS AND RECREATION

BE A RACE CAR DRIVER
FOR THE DAY

Ditch the freeway gridlock and put the pedal to the metal at the Porsche Experience Center in Carson, where you can test the limits of top-of-the-line cars on a specially designed track. The 53-acre grownup playground features a 4-mile handling circuit designed to mimic a heart-stopping drive on a country road. There's also an "ice hill" slick with water jets, an off-road course, and other challenges. The experiences are a bit of a splurge, but a worthwhile investment for car enthusiasts. They also offer a less pricy demo lap with a pro driver, a thrilling option to enjoy as a passenger.

There are also fun options for non-drivers, including a lobby of legendary Porsches, a behind-the-scenes look at the Porsche Motorsports North America workshop, and high-tech driving simulators. And the Porsche 917 Restaurant offers an excellent lineup of seasonal dishes and cocktails, and great views of the driving course.

The Porsche Experience Center
19800 S Main St., Carson 90745

porschedriving.com/porsche-experience-center-los-angeles

Neighborhood: South L.A.
Kid friendly status is up to you, parents.

SKATE THE NIGHT AWAY
AT MOONLIGHT ROLLERWAY

Strap on a pair of roller skates and hit the boards at Glendale's Moonlight Rollerway, one of the last remaining vintage skating rinks in the country. The rink has been a neighborhood landmark for more than 60 years and is a blast for experienced skaters and first-timers. You'll find neon lights, retro carpeting, and disco balls galore. Plus, the flooring is the original 2.5" solid maple wood assembled without nails, a rare feature loved by diehard skaters.

Moonlight Rollerway also has a vintage Hammond B3 organ perched above the rink, played by owner Dominic Cangelosi Tuesday nights. While most rinks replaced live music with DJs and playlists decades ago, the organ creates the perfect throwback sound for skating. Check the calendar for theme nights, including Throwback Thursdays, Family Night on Sundays, and the LGBT-themed Rainbow Night on Wednesdays.

Moonlight Rollerway Skating Rink
5110 San Fernando Rd., Glendale 91204
moonlightrollerway.com

Neighborhood: Glendale
Kid friendly

TAKE AIM
AT A HISTORIC ARCHERY RANGE

Hone your archery skills (or shoot an arrow for the first time) with the Pasadena Roving Archers, a group that offers free archery classes on Saturday mornings in Pasadena's Lower Arroyo, the oldest existing field archery range in the country. For the uninitiated, field archery takes place in both wooded and open terrain where archers shoot at targets of varying sizes and distances on a course of 28 targets. Archers shoot in small groups and move from one target to the next, just like a game of golf. It's a fun and challenging sport that is often compared to martial arts like Tai Chi as it requires both physical precision and mental focus.

The Pasadena Roving Archers classes are open to everyone on Saturday mornings (7 am and 10 am) throughout the year, though the first Saturday of the month is reserved for the City Credential Class. They provide all the archery equipment needed. Be sure to check the website before you go.

Pasadena Roving Archers
415 S Arroyo Blvd., Pasadena 91105
rovingarchers.com

Neighborhood: Pasadena
Kid friendly

NAVIGATE PADDLE BOATS
ON ECHO PARK LAKE

Smack in the middle of the park that gives the neighborhood of Echo Park its name, you'll find a beautiful, palm tree–lined lake. The recently renovated, historic reservoir is not only a great destination for an afternoon stroll, but you can also rent swan-shaped paddle boats and gently cruise around the idyllic lake. The boats are the perfect way to escape the bustle of the city, get a little exercise, and enjoy a romantic escape or a bit of fun with the family. Plus, you can take advantage of picturesque backdrops for selfies, thanks to views of Downtown's skyline, lotus flower blooms, and soaring fountain sprays. The swan boats are available as two-seaters and four-seaters, with the option of a canopy for particularly sunny days. And don't be surprised if you see a marriage proposal or two while you're out on the water.

Wheel Fun Rentals
751 Echo Park Ave., Los Angeles 90026
wheelfunrentals.com/ca/los-angeles/echo-park

Neighborhood: Echo Park
Kid friendly

TIP
Grab breakfast or lunch at Beacon, the grab-and-go restaurant inside of the historic Boathouse next to the rentals.
The wagyu burger is drool-worthy.

HOP ON A BIKE
FOR CITY-WIDE RIDES

While much of L.A. may feel very car-centric, bicycling in the city has become increasingly popular over the past decade thanks to the addition of miles of bike lanes, new bike sharing programs, and special bike-friendly events.

The Passage Ride is for spontaneous souls, adventure-seekers, and those who get a rush out of uncertainty. It's not an athletic event, but you're gonna need sound bicycling chops and more than a beach cruiser. These 20-35-mile late-night bike rides happen every Wednesday night at 9:00 pm and can last until midnight. As you ride across footpaths, over dirt roads, and through alleyways, you'll catch a side of L.A. that few experience. That's the reward for these mysterious routes—well, that and the victory donuts you score after the ride. Be sure to check the website's FAQ section to see if you're up to the challenge, but don't expect a lot of details.

CicLAvia, on the other hand, is more accessible to riders of all skill levels and takes place during the day. There are typically four to five events each year (with plans for more), taking place in different parts of the city, and always on a Sunday. Along the routes, which usually span several miles, there are multiple hubs where participants can rest, hydrate, and enjoy live music and other activities. Seeing the streets of L.A. filled with smiling cyclists, skaters, and pedestrians instead of cars is an incredible experience.

The Passage Ride
Intersection of 3rd/ New Hampshire
Los Angeles 90004
thepassageride.com

CicLAvia
ciclavia.org

Neighborhood:
All over Los Angeles
Kid friendly for CicLAvia;
Adults only for The Passage Ride

GRAB A DODGER DOG AND ROOT
FOR THE HOME TEAM

There are so many heavy-hitters waiting for you at a Dodger game, why wouldn't you get out to watch L.A.'s love affair with their home team in action? (Well that, and those Dodger Dogs awaiting you from inside the gates.) While we'll miss the endearing, familiar voice of Vin Scully calling the game now that he's retired, the stadium will always feel like a second home to some fans. Even if you don't follow baseball closely, it's still a thrill to take a seat in one of the oldest baseball stadiums in the country (only Fenway Park and Wrigley Field have Dodger Stadium beat). Go root for L.A.'s real home team—'cause no matter what they're called officially, those Los Angeles Angels of Anaheim are in Orange County!

Dodger Stadium
1000 Elysian Park Ave., Los Angeles 90012
dodgers.com

Neighborhood: Elysian Park
Kid friendly

TIP

Try scoring tickets to a Friday night home game and plan to stick around after for the impressive fireworks display. They also occasionally have movie nights, so check the schedule.

ZIP DOWN A GLASS SLIDE
70 STORIES ABOVE DTLA

What's better than enjoying jaw-dropping 360-degree views of Los Angeles from California's tallest open-air observation deck? Watching those views zoom past in a blur as you whiz down an outdoor glass slide 1,000 feet in the air. The Skyslide at the OUE Skyspace L.A. is a first-of-its-kind, 45-foot-long glass that takes you from the 70th floor to the 69th floor of the iconic U.S. Bank Tower. While perhaps not for the height-averse, zipping down is a thrilling experience not to be missed. Even if you don't brave the slide, you can still enjoy the views from the observation deck along with interactive exhibits. The OUE Skyspace even offers sunset yoga classes up there, and proposal packages complete with helicopter tours from the roof.

OUE Skyspace L.A.
633 W 5th St., Los Angeles 90071
oue-skyspace.com

Neighborhood: Downtown
Kid friendly

TIP
Consider grabbing a bite at 71Above, the excellent restaurant one floor up serving beautifully presented, upscale fare with those same great views. Save a few bucks by stopping by for lunch or just grab one of their creative cocktails at the bar.

CATCH THEM IF YOU CAN
AT A GRUNION RUN

As strange as it may sound, crowds gather on the shores of various beaches in the South Bay and San Pedro late at night to watch skinny silver fish get romantic and mate on the sand. Weird, right? Actually, it's fascinating. Under the moonlight, in what seems like an instant, the sand turns from brown to silver as the grunion do their deed. After the action, the fish catch the next wave back out to the water and you stand utterly amazed by what you just saw. The grunion are picky and only choose to run on the south-facing beaches of Southern California (and parts of Mexico) during certain times of the year, so mark your calendar and prepare for peak Grunion Run season from late March through early June.

Cabrillo Marine Aquarium
3720 Stephen M. White Dr., San Pedro 90731
cabrillomarineaquarium.org

Neighborhood: San Pedro
Kid friendly

TIP
One of the best and most family friendly places to do a Grunion Run is Cabrillo Beach in San Pedro. Check the Cabrillo Marine Aquarium website for the best information.

HIT
THE BEACH

Sorta obvious, but sometimes you need a break from the concrete jungle. Some beaches are for the scenery, while others are just more about the scene. Here are a few you gotta hit up:

- **El Matador** (Malibu)—Super scenic and very romantic, bring a blanket and catch the sunrise or sunset with your sweetheart.

- **El Porto** (Manhattan Beach)—Can get a little crowded out in the water, but plenty of room for sun bathers. Also, consider a walk or a bike ride on The Strand behind the beach.

- **Hermosa Beach**—The party beach. Lots of people everywhere: in the water, on the sand, and all around town. Less scenic, more scene.

- **Leo Carrillo** (Malibu)—Tide pools, caves, picnic areas, and campsites! Fine for sunbathing, but more for exploring and reflection.

- **Surfrider Beach** (Malibu)—Quintessential Cali beach and the best surfing beach. You'll need experience though; it's not the beach for beginners to hang ten.

- **Zuma Beach** (Malibu)—Quiet, usually not crowded, and picturesque. Sit on the long stretch of white sand and enjoy a solitary moment.

- **Dockweiler State Beach** (Playa Del Rey)—Ideal for families, it's the only beach in the county with fire pits where you can cozy up after a day in the water and roast s'mores. Claim your spot early.

HANG TEN
WITH SURFING LESSONS

With so many fantastic beaches along the coast offering up totally tubular waves, it would be a shame not to hop on a surfboard at least once in L.A. Who knows? You may even get hooked and wind up carving out curls for life. Besides, whether you live in L.A. or are just visiting, people will inevitably ask you if you've ever surfed, so you might as well respond with a "for sure" and a shaka sign (sticking out your thumb and pinkie finger, which roughly translates to "hang loose").

Rather than look like a Barney (amateur) out on the waves, it's a good idea to take a few lessons before you venture out on your own. You'll also enjoy the experience much more once you know what you're doing. Here are a few great schools to get you started.

Pro Surf Instruction with
John Philbin (Malibu)
prosurfinstruction.com

Aloha Brothers (Venice)
alohabrothers.surf

Go Surf L.A. (Santa Monica)
gosurfla.com

TIP

If you're not quite ready to surf, stand up paddle boarding (SUP) is an awesome way to get out in the water, and it's got a much quicker learning curve. Check out SUP with Wade (supwithwade.com) or Venice Paddle Boards (venicepaddleboards.com).

SWIM IN STYLE
AT THE ANNENBERG COMMUNITY BEACH HOUSE

A day spent poolside at the Annenberg Community Beach House will ruin you for life; there's warm sun-kissed water, modern lounge chairs with umbrellas, and sleek outdoor couches in the shade. But the Annenberg trumps any other public pool with the gorgeous Santa Monica beach that's located right behind your lounge chair.

The grounds may look like a *Vogue* magazine cover shoot location, but it's not too-cool-for-school. Everybody gets into the alluring blue water and actually swims! There's a big Mommy and Me scene during the day, so no need to be nervous about coming with kids in tow either.

415 Pacific Coast Hwy., Santa Monica 90402
annenbergbeachhouse.com

Neighborhood: Santa Monica
Kid friendly
Seasonal: May–September

TIP
Make a parking reservation online in advance; it's crucial with such a small lot. You don't wanna walk a half mile down PCH with all your stuff.

SADDLE UP
FOR A SUNSET HORSEBACK RIDE

Calling all romantics (and horse lovers, too)—how does spending four hours on horseback with a 360-degree view of L.A. at sunset sound? You even get to grab a bite to eat and catch a primo view of the Hollywood sign during the ride. Um, this is what memories are made of folks.

In addition to its longer Friday night tour that includes a stop at a Mexican restaurant, Sunset Ranch Hollywood also offers shorter day and evening tours, and a Saturday sunset tour that concludes with BBQ and live country music. Giddy up!

Sunset Ranch Hollywood
3400 North Beachwood Dr., Los Angeles 90068
sunsetranchhollywood.com

Neighborhood: Griffith Park/Los Feliz
Riders must be at least 8 years old

BIKE
THE STRAND

This one is simple: pick any perfect "72-degrees-and-sunny" L.A. day, bust out your bike, and make your way to the Marvin Braude Bike Trail (a.k.a. The Strand). The path is paved and it follows the coastline for 22 miles. If you make it the whole way, you'll have covered almost every beach from the South Bay (Palos Verdes) to Pacific Palisades.

Marvin Braude Bike Trail
Northern end: Will Rogers State Beach, Pacific Palisades
Southern end: Torrance County Beach, Palos Verdes Peninsula

TIP
Don't have a bike? Rent one at any of the major beaches along the path. Hermosa Beach is good if you're starting down south, and Santa Monica works if you're closer to the northern end of the trail.

CRUISE OVER
TO CATALINA ISLAND

Promising a perfect weekend escape, Catalina Island beckons to you from just 22 miles off the L.A. coastline. Why wouldn't you answer the call? There are a few ways to get there (including by helicopter if you're a fan of the movie *Step Brothers*), but the best option is the roughly hour-long ride on the Catalina Express high-speed ferry. Once there, you can rent a bike or golf cart, or just cruise around on foot. Besides just lounging on Descanso Beach (which is totally acceptable), there's plenty to explore. There's the Wrigley Memorial Botanical Garden, the Art Deco Avalon Theatre, hiking on the Trans-Catalina trail, jeep tours to see wild bison, kayak and snorkel excursions, zip-lining, and more. There are also plenty of eateries and bars to check out; just be sure to order up a Buffalo Milk, a boozy milkshake that is Catalina's signature drink. As you'll likely want to stay the night, be sure to book a hotel in advance.

Catalina Express
visitcatalinaisland.com

Neighborhood: Catalina Island
Kid friendly status is all up to you, parents.

TIP
If you visit Catalina Island on your birthday, you can enjoy a free ride with Catalina Express, plus other discounts on the island.

UNWIND AND CUT LOOSE
AT GRAND PARK

Leave it to L.A. to make even a city park stylish. Enjoy some quiet time and reflect on a neon pink park bench or let the kiddos run loose in one of the most dazzling splash pads you've ever seen. Grand Park is so much more than a patch of green amid the grey landscape of Downtown; it's a place to gather and find a sense of community in a crazy busy place. You can also unwind with free yoga classes; hit up food trucks at lunch time; cut loose with dance classes, DJs, and live music; celebrate holidays; and even enjoy a light show in the fountains after dark. It's clean, it's free, it's pet-friendly, it's easily accessible via the Metro, and it really is a grand place to be when in DTLA.

210 N Grand Ave., Los Angeles 90012
grandparkla.org

Neighborhood: Downtown
Kid friendly

CONQUER
THE SECRET STAIRS

Get your gluteus maximus off that Stairmaster; the secret stairs are a far more thrilling (and scenic) workout. These old-school remains are historic evidence that the city wasn't always suffering from gridlock; they used to provide pedestrians with access to trolley cars and railways in the steeper parts of town.

If you conquer the staircase in Beachwood Canyon, not only will you cruise by Humphrey Bogart's and Bela Lugosi's old digs, you'll catch eye-popping views of Downtown, Griffith Park, and Lake Hollywood and earn bragging rights on slaying 861 stairs. You can bust your butt and slam through these in an hour, or you can take your time and soak up all the charms of the hidden Hollywood history throughout the course.

Beachwood Canyon Stairs (start at Beachwood Café)
2695 N Beachwood Dr., Los Angeles 90068
secretstairs-la.com

Neighborhood: Hollywood Hills
Kid friendly status is all up to you, parents.

TIP
Visit Charles Fleming's Secret Stairs L.A. website to download maps or an iPhone app and order books on the dozens of hidden stairways you can conquer all over L.A.

KAYAK DOWN
THE L.A. RIVER

The 51-mile L.A. River has been a hot mess for a long while, but since conservationists have rallied and worked to clean it up, it can now be enjoyed from the cozy hard-plastic confines of a brightly colored kayak. You can even fish from the shores or hike to explore native wildlife. It's best to join a guided kayak expedition for your voyage down the river; along with calm stretches there are also unexpectedly rowdy rapids! You can't row your way through all 51 miles just yet, but the select areas that are designated for "Urban Kayaking" are packed with the kind of beauty (and excitement!) that you would expect from a California outdoor experience.

L.A. River Recreation
lariverrecreation.org

Neighborhood: Central L.A. (Elysian Valley)
Ages 10+
Seasonal: May–September

HIKE TO THE WATERFALL
AT SOLSTICE CANYON

Get up early one weekend (because parking gets crazy) and head to the Santa Monica Mountains to hike Solstice Canyon. The 3-mile loop trail is a peaceful, picturesque escape inside the city's hectic borders. It's gentle enough to bring the kids and dog along, and if you make it the whole way you can explore the ruins of a long-lost mansion and find a waterfall! Since it's not too strenuous or time-consuming, you've got plenty of time left in the day to tackle another item on your bucket list.

Solstice Canyon Park
Corral Canyon Rd., Malibu 90263
everytrail.com/guide/solstice-canyon

Neighborhood: Malibu
Kid friendly

TIP
There are several trails at the park,
including more strenuous routes for more seasoned hikers.

Other Great Hikes To Explore

Mount Hollywood Hike via Charlie Turner's Trail
2800 East Observatory Ave., Los Angeles 90027

Echo Mountain via the Sam Merrill Trail
E Loma Alta Dr. at Lake Ave., Alta Dena 91001

Portuguese Bend Preserve
29800 Crenshaw Blvd., Palos Verdes Peninsula 90275

Eaton Canyon Falls Trail
1750 N Altadena Dr., Pasadena 91107

Malibu Creek State Park via Crags Road
1925 Las Virgenes Rd., Calabasas 91302

Vasquez Rocks
10700 Escondido Canyon Rd., Agua Dulce 91350

CHILL OUT
AT THE HUNTINGTON LIBRARY

Although there are no official statistics proving that your disposition instantly improves and your IQ is automatically heightened upon arriving at The Huntington, there's no doubt you'll feel immediately more cultured and relaxed. With a library, art museum, and botanical gardens all on the same grounds, it's quite the 3-in-1 deal. The Huntington gets major props for the library's big-league collection of literary works, which include an Ellesmere manuscript of *The Canterbury Tales*, a copy of a Gutenberg Bible, and early editions of Shakespeare's work.

However, the botanical gardens throughout the campus are what really draw the crowds. Take your pick from more than a dozen themed areas and just chill out. Whether you find serenity at the Japanese garden, get romantic at the camellia and/or rose gardens, or bring your sketchpad to the lily pad ponds, it's hard to find a more enchanting place to reflect than at The Huntington.

1151 Oxford Rd.
San Marino 91108
huntington.org

Neighborhood:
Pasadena
Kid friendly

TIP
Don't be afraid to bring the kiddos along—
the Children's Garden totally rules!

SPEND A DAY
AT THE RACES

Even if you're not typically a horse racing fan or interested in gambling in the slightest, a visit to the historic Santa Anita Park is an essential L.A. experience. There's nothing quite like cheering on the galloping horses and the jockeys from the 1,100-foot-long Art Deco grandstand with the stunning backdrop of the San Gabriel Mountains.

Grab breakfast at Clocker's Corner, a patio at the top of the stretch where, beginning at 5 am, you can watch the horses train and catch a spectacular sunrise. On Saturday and Sunday mornings, join the Seabiscuit Tour, named for the legendary Santa Anita racehorse. The free tram ride offers of the stables, the jockeys' room, and Seabiscuit's original stall and barn.

Santa Anita also hosts special events throughout the year, including food and beer festivals, live music, and more.

Santa Anita Park
285 Huntington Dr., Arcadia 91007
santaanita.com

Neighborhood: Arcadia
Kid friendly status is up to you, parents.

TIP
Don your finest derby day hat and sharpest blazer, and head up to The Chandelier Room, Santa Anita Park's classy venue with original 1930s chandeliers, live bands, and excellent views of the track from the expansive balcony.

CULTURE AND HISTORY

TIME TRAVEL
IN HISTORIC DTLA

Los Angeles is a city that constantly reinvents itself, but thankfully there are still plenty of historic places to explore, many of which are in Downtown's historic core. There you'll find spectacular architecture, a legendary food hall, and the shortest railway in the world.

Angels Flight
356 S Olive St., Los Angeles 90013

angelsflight.org

This legendary funicular with twin cable cars—Olivet and Sinai—that travel opposite one another, ferries passengers up and down one block of Bunker Hill. First opened in 1901, the orange and black cars of Angels Flight once took Angelenos from the long-gone Victorian mansions to shops and theaters below. Thanks to a recent renovation, you can catch a ride on this piece of history.

Grand Central Market

317 S Broadway, Los Angeles 90013
grandcentralmarket.com

Feast on a huge variety of delicious eats from new vendors and legacy tenants for breakfast, lunch, and now dinner. Try classics like carnitas tacos from Villa Moreliana, Salvadorian pupusas from Sarita's, and wonton soup from China Café. And try new eats like the burger at Belcampo Meat Co., Thai food at Sticky Rice, falafel at Madcapra, and pastrami from Wexler's Deli. And if you have time for the long line, breakfast sandwiches at Eggslut.

Bradbury Building

304 S Broadway, Los Angeles 90013
thebradbury.com

After chowing at Grand Central Market, head across Broadway to the oldest commercial building in the area, which opened in 1893. Travel back in time with marble staircases, detailed iron railings, open cage elevators. and light pouring in from the glass ceiling above. The interior has been used in numerous films, including *Blade Runner, (500) Days of Summer,* and *The Artist.*

Neighborhood: Downtown
Kid friendly

HOP ON A JEEPNEY TOUR
OF HISTORIC FILIPINOTOWN

Climb aboard a colorfully decorated, open-air jeep to discover the rich culture, history, and delicious food of L.A.'s vibrant Filipino community. Los Angeles is home to one of the country's biggest populations of Filipino Americans, and yet many visitors and locals aren't as familiar with the neighborhood of Historic Filipinotown (a.k.a. Hi Fi) as they are other ethnic enclaves such as Koreatown or Little Ethiopia. The Hidden Hi Fi Jeepney tours, organized by the Pilipino Workers Center, plan to change that with fun, interactive expeditions aboard a rare and vintage 1944 Sarao Motor Company Jeepney—a hand-painted, elaborately decorated military jeep that has been a popular form of public transportation in the Philippines since World War II. The lively tours are the perfect way to learn about the community and introduce you to tasty Filipino treats like ube (sweet purple yam) ice cream.

Hidden Hi Fi
pwcsc.org/hiddenhifi-la/

Neighborhood: Historic Filipinotown
Kid friendly

Los Angeles is at the forefront of the growing popularity of Filipino cuisine in the U.S., often referred to as the Filipino Food Movement, and you can dig into delicious eats at old school spots and new destinations. Here are just some of our favorites:

L.A. Rose Cafe
4749 Fountain Ave.
Los Angeles 90029
Long-running favorite for classic Filipino cuisine in a cozy setting with live music and excellent empanadas. For breakfast, get the garlic rice and eggs with longanisa (Filipino pork sausage).

Rice Bar
419 W 7th St.
Los Angeles 90014
Celebrated chef Charles Olalia's intimate spot for modern takes on traditional rice dishes as well as turmeric adobo (vinegar braised pork belly), chicken tinola (ginger-papaya broth), and crispy spam and eggs.

Bahay Kubo
2330 W Temple St.
Los Angeles 90026
Head to the tropical-themed patio of this Historic Filipinotown spot for inexpensive home-style Filipino cooking like BBQ pork skewers and kare kare, a hearty stew with a savory peanut sauce.

LASA
727 N Broadway
Los Angeles 90012
Brothers Chad and Chase Valencia are serving up some of the most exciting, progressive Filipino cuisine in the country, which incorporates seasonal California ingredients like lumpia sariwa (spring rolls with black kale and butternut squash) and crispy duck leg tinola with braised chayote.

The Park's Finest
1267 W Temple St.
Los Angeles 90026
This Historic Filipinotown destination serves creative Filipino twists on American BBQ such as coconut beef, hot links with longanisa, and cornbread bibingka (a banana leaf–wrapped cake).

FrankieLucy Bakeshop
3116 Sunset Blvd.
Los Angeles 90026
Indulge your sweet tooth at this coffee shop with colorful treats like pandan (young coconut) chia pudding, mango crème caramel, and ube (purple yam) upside down pie. Don't miss the ube horchata with a shot of espresso.

FIND YOUR INNER BOHEMIAN
AT TOPANGA CANYON

Maybe you've never yearned to have your chakras aligned or donned a pair of roman sandals, but once you're up in Topanga Canyon, you'll want to twirl around with flowers in your hair. It's a hideaway in between the majesty of Malibu and the plush Pacific Palisades that's too gorgeous to go unexplored. True nature in L.A. is scarce, so get out there and do a little hiking (or perhaps an impromptu yoga session?); you've got many trails and paths to choose from.

At the very least, stop by the Inn of the Seventh Ray and browse the bookstore. After you spot the woodland dining room though, you won't want to leave—surrender and stay for lunch or book reservations for dinner. It's one heck of a place for a wedding proposal too, if you wanted to take things to another level …

Inn of the Seventh Ray
128 Old Topanga Canyon Rd., Topanga 90290
innoftheseventhray.com

Neighborhood: Topanga
Kid friendly status is all up to you, parents.

GO BEHIND-THE-SCENES
AT A NASA RESEARCH CENTER

Forget the stars of Hollywood and take an inside look at the stellar studies of NASA's Jet Propulsion Laboratory (JPL) in Pasadena, the leading U.S. center for robotic exploration of the solar system. The 177-acre JPL campus is where more than 5,000 scientists and other workers design, build, and study interplanetary spacecraft, including satellites and other robotic space craft like rovers and landers. JPL offers free tours to the public where visitors have the unique opportunity to get a behind-the-scenes view of JPL's mission control room, the dust-free vehicle assembly hangar, a museum of JPL's missions, and more. Tour reservations must be made at least three weeks in advance, though they can often book up to six months out, so plan accordingly.

Jet Propulsion Laboratory
4800 Oak Grove Dr., Pasadena 91109

Neighborhood: Pasadena
Kid friendly

LEARN THE LORE OF L.A.'s UNDERBELLY
WITH ESOTOURIC

Beneath the glitz and glamour that many people associate with the City of Angels lies a dark history of grit, crime, and mischief. Dive into the dark side with Esotouric's bus tours, which traverse the city covering everything from true crime tales and literary legends to endangered architectural gems and forgotten histories. Led by preservationists Kim Cooper and Richard Schave, these are not your typical snooze-fest history lessons or bus tours of movie stars' homes. Find out where Bukowski wrote (and drank), see the locations that inspired the novels of James M. Cain and Raymond Chandler, and see if you can solve the mystery of the infamous Black Dahlia murder.

Esotouric
esotouric.com

Neighborhood: All over L.A.
Adults only (maybe older kids)

TIP
Download Kim and Richard's podcast *You Can't Eat The Sunshine* to learn more about the forgotten histories of L.A.

SLEEP OVER
AT THE LA BREA TAR PITS

It's crazy enough that these smelly, gooey tar pits exist right in the middle of the city, but when the kids get a flashlight-guided tour through them after dark, they're likely to have the time of their lives—and parents might enjoy the scavenger hunt throughout the museum by night as well. Kids must be 5 or older, and they need a parent to accompany them on their adventure.

If excavated Ice-Age bones and gooey artifacts aren't your thing, you can also do a sleepover at the Natural History Museum. The museum also hosts adults-only slumber parties complete with a bar, DJs, scavenger hunts, and midnight movie screenings.

Page Museum at the La Brea Tar Pits
5801 Wilshire Blvd., Los Angeles 90036
nhm.org/site/activities-programs/overnight-adventures

Neighborhood: Miracle Mile
Kid friendly

GET A
LITTLE RELIGION

Perhaps Los Angeles isn't best known for its spiritual side, but there sure are some major power players in the City of Angels. If you're curious,people flock to several places of worship in L.A. daily, whether it's just to gawk or to enlighten.

• **Cathedral of Our Lady of Angels** (Downtown)—Arguably the most famous church in L.A., the cathedral features architecture that draws in as many tourists as the Catholic faith does.

• **Church of Scientology** (Hollywood)—With its long roster of celebrity members, it's fitting that Scientology's flagship property is located in Hollywood. Go see for yourself what the controversy is all about.

• **Hsi Lai Temple** (Hacienda Heights)—Covering 15 acres, this Buddhist temple is the largest Chinese Temple in the United States. Tourists are welcomed, and audio tours are available. There's even a vegetarian buffet lunch served from 11-1 every day in the cafeteria.

• **Mission San Fernando Rey de España** (San Fernando Valley) and **Mission San Gabriel** (San Gabriel Valley)—The California Missions have been a mainstay in L.A. culture for centuries, and these are two of the twenty-one missions located within Los Angeles County.

- **Los Angeles California Temple** (Westwood)—You may need card-carrying credentials to tour this Mormon temple thoroughly, but anyone can get a free tour of the visitor center and take pictures of this stunning temple from the outside.
- **Wilshire Boulevard Temple** (Koreatown)—L.A. has long been home to a large, thriving Jewish community; visit the first synagogue in Los Angeles and its newly restored sanctuary.

Neighborhood: All over Los Angeles
Kid friendly

TIPTOE THROUGH
SECRET GARDENS

Hidden away from the bustling streets and concrete sprawl of L.A. are some magical secret gardens that offer refreshing respite for those who know where to look. These idyllic patches of green are perfect for calming the mind, reconnecting with nature, and generally just taking a break from tromping around the city. Here are some of our favorites:

James Irvine Japanese Garden (Little Tokyo)
jaccc.org
jamesirvinejapanesegarden/
This sunken garden is inspired by the Zen gardens of Kyoto and features a cascading stream, cedar bridges, and beautifully manicured greenery.

Peace Awareness Labyrinth & Gardens (Jefferson Park)
peacelabyrinth.org
Challenge your spacial intelligence and find peace while walking the labyrinth, wandering the gardens, and touring the historic Guasti Villa.

Self-Realization Fellowship Lake Shrine (Pacific Palisades)
lakeshrine.org
Wander the lush gardens and lake of this sprawling meditation retreat where a portion of Mahatma Gandhi's ashes are enshrined.

Amir's Garden (Griffith Park)
amirsgarden.org
Created single-handedly by Amir Dialameh over three decades, this five-acre garden is now maintained by volunteers and is a great rest stop for hikers in Griffith Park.

Neighborhood: All over Los Angeles
Kid friendly

MEET A MASTER
CRAFTSMAN

Forget the Bel Air mansions, California Craftsman houses are some of the most envied and aspirational in all of L.A. The Gamble House in Pasadena is not only a real looker, but it's actually considered to be the masterpiece of the entire American Arts & Crafts movement—BOOM! With those kinds of credentials, set aside some time to visit this exquisite home built in 1909 for David Gamble (of Procter & Gamble fame). It's truly amazing to see how something built so long ago still holds up to today's modern standards and tastes. Definitely pony up for the docent-led tour; you can't possibly see what all the fuss is about unless you've gone inside the house, too.

4 Westmoreland Pl., Pasadena 91103
gamblehouse.org

Neighborhood: Pasadena
Kid friendly, but you be the judge.
(It's a historical landmark, perhaps not ideal for frisky toddlers)

FUN FACT
Look familiar? You may recognize the house as
Doc Brown's mansion in *Back to the Future*!

EXPLORE AN
ABANDONED ZOO

Wandering through an abandoned zoo may sound like the stuff of nightmares to some, but trust us, exploring the remnants of the Old L.A. Zoo is a worthwhile adventure (even if it is a bit eerie). The zoo first opened in 1912 with many of the enclosures added in the 1930s, before it was abandoned in 1966 for its current home further north in Griffith Park (that zoo is also worth a visit). While some enclosures were removed, many remain, including the lions' den, bear grottos, and monkey cages. It's an incredible time warp to imagine a zoo-goer's experience from decades ago and to see just how small those cages were. There's also a short hiking trail and a picnic area to enjoy as part of the visit. To get there, head towards the merry-go-round on Crystal Springs Drive and look for signs for the Old L.A. Zoo off Griffith Park Drive.

Neighborhood: Griffith Park
Kid friendly (for the brave)

TIP
During the summer, check out performances by the Independent Shakespeare Co. (iscla.org/griffith-park-festival/) on the lawn in front of the Old Zoo, and around Halloween, check out the Haunted Hayride (losangeleshauntedhayride.com) there, too.

SEE REAL STARS
AT THE GRIFFITH OBSERVATORY

It's easy to forget that celebrities aren't the only stars in Los Angeles, so hit the Griffith Observatory to remind you what the real ones look like. Since they're open Tuesday through Sunday until 10:00 pm, go late and head upstairs to the rooftop dome for a stellar view with the giant Zeiss telescope (it's free!). If you like stargazing that's more social, attend the "star parties" held by the Los Angeles Astronomical Society and Sidewalk Astronomers once a month. Or, rely on your naked eye and do an evening hike on a clear night under the stars—there are plenty of hiking trails to try in Griffith Park. Don't disregard it because of its high tourist appeal; there's a reason why people get so starry-eyed over the Observatory.

2800 E. Observatory Ave., Los Angeles 90027
griffithobs.org

Neighborhood: Griffith Park/Los Feliz
Kid friendly

INVESTIGATE THE
UNDERGROUND TUNNELS OF DTLA

Beneath the streets of Downtown L.A. hides a vast network of secret subterranean tunnels just waiting to be explored. Generally closed to the public, the 11-mile network of underground passageways of service tunnels, abandoned subway lines, and old equestrian paths can now be investigated thanks to Cartwheel Art Tours and Hotel Indigo. The tours, led by writer/historian Sandi Hemmerlein, take urban explorers through the century-old tunnels that have been used for transporting everything from prisoners by police to cash by banks and booze by smugglers during Prohibition. During the tour, you'll learn all about the notorious history of the tunnels and peer inside old speakeasies used by revelers during Prohibition.

Cartwheel Art Tours
cartwheelart.com

Neighborhood: Downtown
Kid friendly status up to you, parents.

SEEK SCENIC SOLACE
AT THE WAYFARERS CHAPEL

If you're in search of a spectacularly stunning setting for a wedding or just a phenomenal backdrop for a photo, look no further than the Wayfarers Chapel. Perched high above the Pacific on the rocky cliffs of Rancho Palos Verdes, the ethereal-looking chapel is constructed of redwood struts and beams and large geometric glass panes for the walls and ceiling. It's truly stunning to see, especially with a deep blue sky above or at sunset. Designed by Lloyd Wright, son of the renowned architect Frank Lloyd Wright, the chapel was the vision of Elizabeth Shellenberg, a member of the Swedenborgian Church, and was completed in 1951. Obviously, the chapel is a popular wedding destination (couples have just two hours to get in and out), but it's open to the public to visit as long as there are no services taking place at the time.

Wayfarers Chapel
5755 Palos Verdes Dr. S, Rancho Palos Verdes 90275
wayfarerschapel.org

Neighborhood: Rancho Palos Verdes
Kid friendly

CELEBRATE JAPANESE AMERICAN HISTORY
AT NISEI WEEK

The explosive colors, exquisite pageantry, and annual traditions of the nine-day celebration in Little Tokyo known as Nisei Week make it fascinating, but the anime cosplay contest, street vendors, and Grand Parade make it fun. There's also a baby show on a mini train (adorable), a gyoza eating championship (delicious), a karate tournament (impressive), and more. Held in August, the festivities started in 1934 when 1st generation Japanese immigrants wanted to keep the culture alive for the 2nd generation (Nisei), but today everyone enjoys this explosion of awesomeness. Bring a folding chair if you can—the parade is lengthy, but as long as you stocked up on those special sweet treats only available during Nisei Week each year, you'll be all set.

Nisei Week Grand Parade
Central Ave. and 2nd St., Los Angeles 90012
niseiweek.org

Neighborhood: Little Tokyo
Kid friendly

STEP INSIDE HISTORY
AT HERITAGE SQUARE

Many of the beautifully ornate Victorian Era homes that once dotted the Los Angeles landscape have since been demolished, but there's one place where you can experience what life was like at the turn of the 19th century. Heritage Square Museum is a living history museum where you can explore nine buildings (plus a vintage train and trolley car) that showcase the range of architectural styles from the 1850s to the early decades of the 20th century. In addition to guided tours and exhibits, there are also special living history events like a Holiday Lamplight Celebration, lectures and demonstrations on death and mourning rituals at Halloween, musical performances, silent movie screenings, and even gardening days to learn about Victorian Era kitchen gardens.

Heritage Square Museum
3800 Homer St., Montecito Heights 90031
heritagesquare.org

Neighborhood: Montecito Heights
Kid friendly

CLIMB ABOARD
THE HAUNTED *QUEEN MARY*

Head down to Long Beach to explore the historic *Queen Mary*, a retired ocean liner that sailed the seas from 1936 to 1967 and is considered one of the most haunted places in the U.S. Not only did the stylish vessel carry celebrities, dignitaries, and royalty during its heyday, but it was also used to transport troops during WWII. These days the Queen Mary is a popular destination for everything from paranormal and historic tours to live local music and seasonal festivities. It also has multiple dining options and bars—including a swank 1930s Art Deco cocktail lounge—and you can even spend the night in one of the luxurious staterooms to get a feel for what transatlantic travel was like during the early 19th century.

The *Queen Mary*
1126 Queens Hwy., Long Beach 90802
queenmary.com

Neighborhood: Long Beach
Kid friendly (for some activities)

STROLL ALONG
THE HISTORIC VENICE CANALS

Before you book a flight to Italy, make a point to explore L.A.'s very own Venice Canals. Opened to the public in 1905, developer Abbot Kinney (yes, the namesake of the trendy boulevard) transformed saltwater marshland into a resort destination with a grand network of waterways and pedestrian bridges. Originally, the "Venice of America" featured seven wide canals and a large lagoon, and tourists and residents could travel by boat (including singing gondoliers!), by footpath, or a miniature train(!). Sadly, the grand vision succumbed to the rising popularity of the automobile, and the canals were filled in and paved over beginning in 1929. Fortunately for us, the Short Line canals—a smaller network built just after Kinney's—survived. So, continue past the circus of the Venice boardwalk and enjoy a leisurely stroll along the picturesque canals, over the footbridges, and past charming cottages and funky architecture. It's a uniquely L.A. experience not to be missed.

Neighborhood: Venice
Kid friendly

TIP
In early December, be sure to check out the Venice Canals Holiday Boat Parade, when residents deck out their canoes, kayaks, and small boats with festive lights and decorations and cruise along the canals. Homes and bridges are also decorated, so it's always a bright and colorful time to visit.

PAL AROUND
AT THE KOREAN BELL OF FRIENDSHIP

This underrated spot often gets overlooked, but with its expansive views of the entire L.A. Harbor alongside the seascapes of San Pedro, it's a great spot to sip a latte and catch up with a cherished compadre. The bell is one big daddy (it weighs 17 tons and stands 12 feet tall), but it's the massive and intricately designed pagoda structure that will stop you in your tracks. You don't need to spend half the day there, but sharing a special moment with a long-time pal is the perfect way to honor this colossal gift of friendship from the Republic of Korea.

Korean Bell of Friendship and Bell Pavilion at Angel's Gate
Recreation Center
3601 S Gaffey St., San Pedro 90731

Neighborhood: San Pedro
Kid friendly

More Places To Explore In San Pedro

CRAFTED at The Port of Los Angeles
(Locally made artisanal goods)
112 E 22nd St.
craftedportla.com

Cabrillo Marine Aquarium
(Frank Gehry-designed building with SoCal
marine life)
3720 Stephen M. White Dr.
cabrillomarineaquarium.org

Brouwerij West
(Belgian-inspired craft beer)
110 E 22nd St.
brouwerijwest.com

Sunken City
(A neighborhood that tumbled down to the beach,
just past that fence…)
500 W Paseo Del Mar

Battleship USS *IOWA*
(Massive maritime museum)
250 S Harbor Blvd.
pacificbattleship.com

Busy Bee Market
(Fantastic deli sandwiches)
2413 S Walker Ave.
busybeemarket.juisyfood.com

FLUTTER THROUGH
THE BUTTERFLY PAVILION

L.A.'s Natural History Museum is a hot spot for sure, but if you can swing it, try and plan your visit sometime between April and September when the Butterfly Pavilion is on view. Rather than peering through glass to see two butterflies hiding somewhere in the back of a small terrarium, you get a chance to walk through the natural habitat where several varieties of native and subtropical butterflies will surround you. The exhibit is quite popular, but since all tickets come with a time reservation, your experience inside can be pretty intimate. Instagram addicts will go nuts, as it's almost like the butterflies just sit there and pose for you.

900 Exposition Blvd., Los Angeles 90007
nhm.org

Neighborhood: South LA
Kid friendly

TIP

The NHM also offers several excellent after-hours programs for grown-ups that are definitely worth checking out. From February to June, check out First Fridays, featuring guest lectures, live music, DJs, food and drink, and tours. And on select dates in July and August, catch Summer Nights in the Garden with garden-inspired cocktails, DJs, live performances, animal meet-and-greets, and more.

SHOPPING AND FASHION

HUNT FOR TREASURE
AT THE ROSE BOWL FLEA MARKET

This is like the Boston Marathon for shopaholics, thrifters, and general bargain seekers—and held in a stadium as famous as The Rose Bowl, you had better believe it's just as epic. The hunting and haggling has been going down every 2nd Sunday of the month since 1967, and if you plan on going, you can't mess around. Get there early, bring (a ton of) cash, and prepare to walk for days knowing you may not even cover half of it. It sounds rough, but treasures from just about every decade are waiting to be found, and bargaining the price is always an option. Oh, and what other flea market do you know of with a wine stand? You're gonna need a whole day for this.

1001 Rose Bowl Dr., Pasadena 91103
rgcshows.com/rosebowl.aspx

Neighborhood: Pasadena
Kid friendly
2nd Sunday of the month, rain or shine

GET LOST IN A LABYRINTH OF LITERATURE
AT THE LAST BOOKSTORE

While many of us often read words on a screen more often than paper these days, we're grateful that there are still a few remaining bookstores offering the print option, including an incredible one in Downtown L.A. The Last Bookstore is part new and used book shop, part record store, part gallery, and a totally captivating community space launched by book lover Josh Spencer. Located in a former bank building, the 22,000-square-foot space is a sight to behold: two stories with rows upon rows of books and enchanting sculptures made with books. Carve out plenty of time to peruse the maze of bookshelves, including the Art & Rare Book Annex and the second floor of $1 books, former vaults, and art galleries. The store also hosts great events, including author readings and musical performances.

453 S Spring St., Los Angeles 90013
lastbookstorela.com

Neighborhood: Downtown
Kid friendly

RISE AND SHINE
AT THE ORIGINAL L.A. FLOWER MARKET

Get up early one morning and head out to the Flower District. You'd never guess the bright colors, fresh smells, and hustle and bustle of the crowds could elicit such excitement. Florists and the general public have been flocking to the Original Los Angeles Flower Market since 1919 and to the adjacent Southern California Flower Market since 1912, and you should participate at least once. The flowers and plants are ridiculously inexpensive, and it's just a buck to get in on Saturdays. Avoid Fridays—that's a serious day with all the florists and DIY wedding planners who are there frantically stocking up—but any other day is a great one to stop and smell the roses … or chrysanthemums … or daisies.

754 Wall St., Los Angeles 90014
originallaflowermarket.com

Neighborhood: Downtown
Kid friendly, but not ideal if shopping with small children

TIP
Stop by Poppy + Rose, the charming café on the street between the two markets, to fuel up before or after you shop. Inspired by classic country kitchens, they've got excellent fried chicken and waffles, biscuits, and other great brunch and lunch items.

SHOP AND EAT
ON L.A.'s VERY FIRST STREET

Downtown's Olvera Street is regarded by many as L.A.'s first street and the birthplace of the city, and the block-long, brick-lined street is a charming, living museum well worth a visit. Created in 1930 to preserve the past, the tree-shaded street features small stalls selling Mexican folk art, pottery, leather goods, toys, and more, as well as Avila Adobe, L.A.'s oldest house. Throughout the year, you'll also encounter festive celebrations showcasing mariachi bands and traditional folk dancing, including the Blessing of the Animals, Dia de Los Muertos, and Mexican Independence Day. Grab a bite of traditional Mexican fare at La Golondrina Mexican Café, and don't miss the world-famous taquitos in avocado sauce at Cielito Lindo, serving since 1934.

125 Paseo de La Plaza, Los Angeles 90012
elpueblo.lacity.org

Neighborhood: Downtown
Kid friendly

TIP
After exploring Olvera Street, be sure to check out some of the other nearby historical sites and museums, including the Sepulveda House, La Plaza de Cultura y Artes, The Pico House, the Chinese American Museum, the Italian American Museum of Los Angeles, and Union Station.

SUGGESTED
ITINERARIES

VINTAGE L.A.

COCKTAILS, PLEASE!

MUSEUM DAY

FAMILY FIELD TRIPS

FOR THE MUSIC LOVERS

FREE STUFF

ACTIVITIES
BY SEASON

Despite L.A.'s sunny year-round weather, there are still
activities reserved for specific times of the year.
This is a quick portrait of some of those seasonal events:

WINTER

Camp Out Before the Rose Parade, 76

Hike to a Waterfall at Solstice Canyon, 100

Experience Cinema's Golden Age at Historic Movie Palaces, 54

Climb aboard the Haunted *Queen Mary*, 124

Skate the Night Away at Moonlight Rollerway, 83

SPRING

Picnic on the Grass at The Getty Center, 77

Bike The Strand, 95

Chill Out at the Huntington Library, 102

Flutter through Butterfly Pavilion, 128

Catch a Flick at the Hollywood Forever Cemetery, 61

Catch Them If You Can at a Grunion Run, 90

Tiptoe through Secret Gardens, 116

SUMMER

FALL

INDEX